SAILING BARGES

OF THE BRITISH ISLES

SAILING BARGES

OF THE BRITISH ISLES

MICHAEL STAMMERS

In memory of the late Edward Paget-Tomlinson, mentor and friend

First published 2008

The History Press
Cirencester Road, Chalford,
Stroud, Gloucestershire, GL6 8PE
www.thehistorypress.co.uk

British Library Cataloguing in Publication Data.
A catalogue record for this book is available from the British Library.

ISBN 978 0 7524 4623 3

Printed in Great Britain by Ashford Colour Press Ltd.

CONTENTS

ACKNOWLEDGEMENTS

As this is a work of compression and summary, the works I have consulted can be found listed in the bibliography. The illustrations are credited at the end of their captions, and in addition I must thank the following people for their help: Peter Barton on the Tees; John Buglass and Mike Clarke on Humber keel wrecks; Valerie Fenwick for help with ancient barges and those on the River Rother; Captain George Hogg on West Country barges; Michael McCaughan of the Ulster Folk and Transport Museum on Irish barges, especially those on the Lagan; Michael Nash of Marine & Cannon Books for access to his photograph and postcard collection; Dr Michael Nix of Glasgow Museums for digging out new evidence on the gabberts of the Clyde; Owain Roberts for his help on Welsh barges; Pamela Paget-Tomlinson for allowing me to use the late Edward Paget-Tomlinson's splendid drawings; Adrian Osler for generously sharing new research to ensure a more nuanced and authoritative account of the Tyne keels and wherries, as well as allowing me to reproduce his drawings of the Tyne keel and wherry.

1

ARCHAEOLOGY, RECORDS AND PICTURES

Let's be clear from the start about what kind of barge this book is all about. The word 'barge' has several meanings. It appears to derive from the Latin *Barca* which has gone down two routes to provide us with barge and barque or bark. In the Middle Ages a barge was a substantial rowing and sailing vessel. In fourteenth-century England, a typical barge was between 200 and 300 tons (*Sherborne, 1994*). The barge *Salvator* of 1445, which belonged to the Bishop of St Andrews, measured 500 tons (*Forte, 1998*). In the succeeding centuries, the word also came to mean a rowing vessel that carried kings, princes and high officials. Prince Frederick's barge at the National Maritime Museum is a wonderful surviving example of this type of ceremonial barge. This was built in 1731–2 for Frederick, Prince of Wales, the eldest son of George II. It was 63ft long by only 6ft beam and was rowed by a crew of sixteen oarsmen. Alexander Kent, who was one of the leading architects of the time, designed a suite of carvings that decorated the vessel from stem to stern (*Norton, 1972*).

The term barge was also used for a specific size of warship's boat which was reserved for the personal use of a flag officer. It was longer and lighter than a pinnace and measured about 32ft and never rowed with less than ten oars (*May, 1999*). The National Maritime Museum has models of this type of admiral's barge and a full-size French one belongs to the Irish National Museum in Dublin. This was abandoned after the failure of the French attack on Bantry Bay in 1797. It measured just over 38ft long and carried three sails in addition to its oars.

While such stately eighteenth-century taxis were carrying their important owners, more rough-and-ready flat-bottomed barges were busy carrying all kinds of cargoes. Hoys and spritsail barges were working in their hundreds on the Thames; keels were ferrying coal down the Tyne; Mersey flats were bringing salt from Cheshire; Severn trows were distributing goods along the length of the Welsh borders; and there were other cargo barges on waterways elsewhere in the British Isles. And these barges were no first generation, for barges had been plying inshore and inland waters for centuries. They were indeed part of a rich and varied heritage of British vernacular boats.

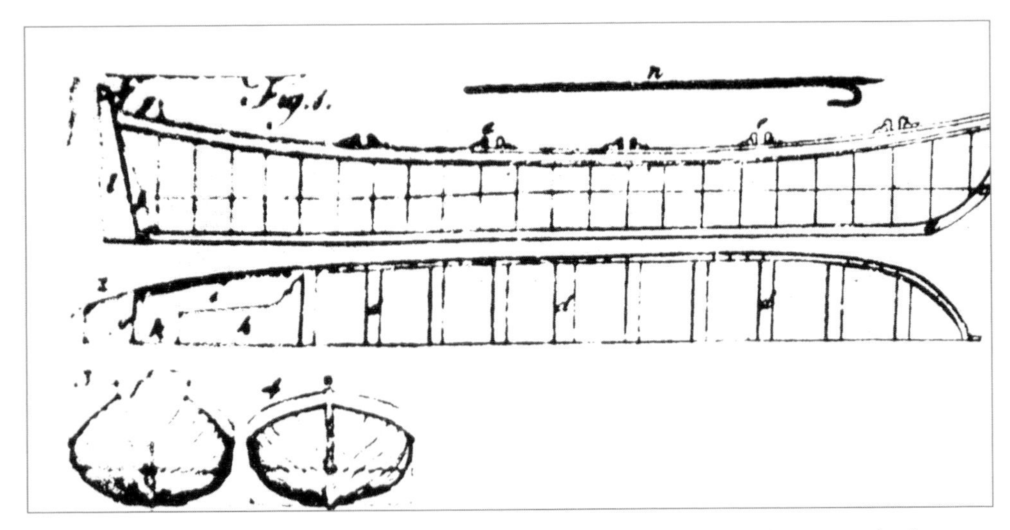

A warship's barge from Falconer's *Marine Dictionary* of 1780 – the same name but a completely different kind of boat to commercial sailing barges.

Cargo-carrying sailing barges have been used around the Thames and Severn estuaries for almost 2,000 years and possibly longer. The overall picture of sailing barge usage remains frustratingly incomplete until the last two centuries. The waterlogged remains of wooden boats or barges can remain stable for long periods, sealed in the aerobic silt of a waterfront shore. They are usually revealed by accident as a result of some civil engineering operation on a waterfront. Such timbers often get exposed well into the work programme. This means that they have been partly destroyed and are often incomplete in vital details. They are also difficult to excavate systematically in order to extract the greatest possible information from them. This is because there is often pressure not to delay the original engineering works, by placing a time limit on their recording and removal. The conditions – usually down a deep, muddy hole – are often difficult, and the timbers need to be removed as soon as possible to stop them drying out, shrinking and distorting. After that, the conservation process to stabilise them is long and expensive.

The remains of a number of flat-bottomed sailing barges that date back to the second and third centuries AD have been excavated in the last 100 years. The rebuilding of the embankment along the Thames in the area of the old Roman city has yielded several wrecks and fragments from Roman to Medieval times. Among the earliest and most barge-like are the remains of 37ft of the bottom and port side of a Romano-British vessel found at Blackfriars in 1962. When complete, Blackfriars Boat No.1 would have measured just over 60ft long with a beam of 20ft. It was carvel built with a flat bottom with two heavy keel planks running along its centre line to provide its structural strength. It had closely spaced heavy oak floor and side timbers fashioned from naturally curved crooks, and the planking was fastened to these by long iron nails driven through treenails and then clenched over into the tops of the frames. The gaps between the planks were caulked with a mixture of pine resin and shavings of hazel wood. A rather worn coin dating from 88 or 89 AD was probably a good luck offering because it was found under the mast step. The position of this feature suggested that this barge was rigged with a single square sail. There was little evidence that

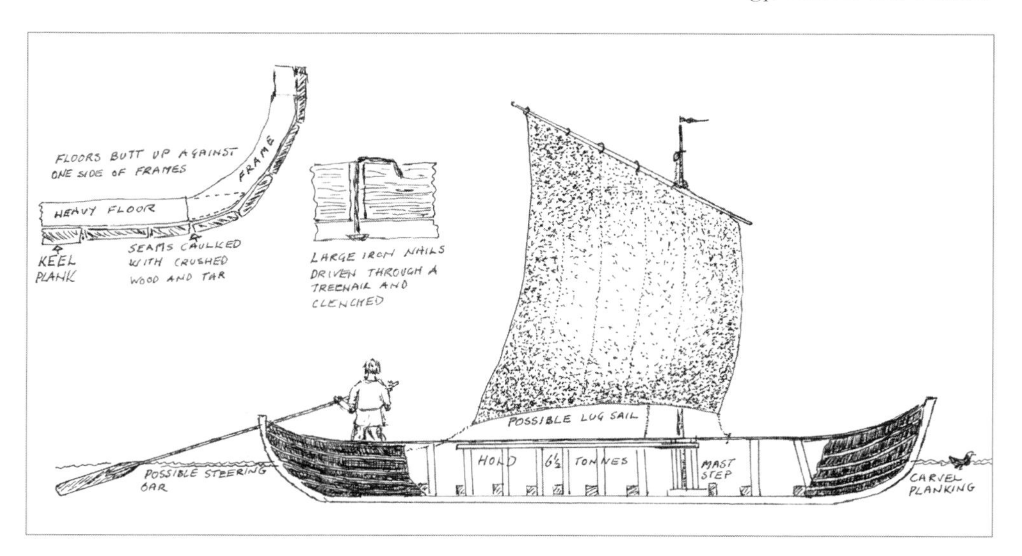

A reconstruction of the Barlands Farm barge, based on the model by Owain Roberts.

it was built with decks or deck beams and slight evidence for decks. It sank with a cargo of 26 tons of Kentish ragstone which may have been loaded on the Medway near Maidstone. The height of the cargo suggested that it had a depth of hold of about 5ft 6in. Some of its planking shows signs of being attacked by marine boring worms which implied that it made more sea voyages and not just short trips (*Delgado, 1997: 64*).

The Barlands Farm Boat is another barge from the Roman occupation and has been dated using dendrochronology to the third century AD. Barlands Farm, near Magor, Gwent, lies 2 miles inland from the present foreshore. The barge was found during the preparation of the site for a new supermarket distribution centre in 1993. The remains were found in what must have been an old creek (or locally a 'pill') leading to the Severn estuary. All the surviving timbers were fashioned from oak. They consisted of a wide plank-keel made up from two thick planks about 23ft long, the lower part of the stem post, much of the of framing which consisted of floor timbers and overlapping side timbers. Incidentally, this form of framing was found in some later barges such as nineteenth-century Mersey flats. It would be difficult to prove that there was a continuous tradition of building frames in this way. It was a just a sound and economical solution for joining the flat bottom planks to the sides. There were also some bottom planks and side strakes (planks) and, crucially, a mast step, a third of the waterline length from the bow. The timbers were fastened in a similar way to Blackfriars No.1, and it has been argued that these two finds, along with similar ones of around the same date, are evidence of a 'Romano-Celtic' tradition of boat building that may have pre-dated the Roman invasion (*McGrail, 1995: 139–145*).

When built, it would have measured just over 37ft long with a beam of 10ft 3in. As the mast step was positioned well forward, it probably carried a lugsail. Computer analysis of the properties of the hull demonstrated that it would have sailed easily and could have carried up to six tons of cargo. This would be the equivalent of fifteen barrels of wine, ninety sacks of grain or fifty sheep (*Roberts and McGrail, 2002: 32–36*). A fine model of the barge under sail is on display at the Newport Museum, and it is also hoped to display the original timbers in the same gallery once they are conserved.

Stern view of the model on show at Newport Museum and Gallery. (Owain Roberts)

Clinker building was another technique for barge building. It consists of building a hull up from overlapping planks fastened together around a keel, stem and stern posts. The strengthening frames were installed after the outer shell of planking had been finished. It was widely used among the peoples of northern Europe in the early centuries AD, and was probably introduced into Britain by settlers arriving around the time of the gradual disintegration of the Roman province of Britannia in the fifth century. Clinker-built boats of that post-Roman period are popularly associated with warships and burial rituals, from Sutton Hoo in Suffolk in the seventh century to Gokstad, Norway, in the tenth century. But there were more humble types of fishing boat and cargo ship constructed in the same way. This continued right through to the early twentieth century when Norfolk wherries (to take just one barge example) were still being built from overlapping planks.

The redevelopment of the City of London's waterfront during the 1960s and 1970s uncovered the remains of three Thames barges – two from the fifteenth century and one from

The Buck brothers' views of the Thames showed swim-headed sailing barges which also appear to be medieval in origin.

the 1680s. Blackfriars III was a sailing barge built around 1400 and measured approximately 46ft by 13ft. It was double-ended, clinker built in oak and without any form of deck. It was probably rigged with a single square sail. Blackfriars IV lay close by and may have collided with Blackfriars III. It was a smaller vessel, possibly a lighter for ferrying cargo to and from ships at anchor in the Pool. It was a similar design to III, though with much lighter timbers. Only a cross-section of this barge could be recorded because of the constraints of safety, and its beam measured between 10–11ft. Blackfriars II was a barge dating from about 1680 which was lost while carrying a cargo of bricks. Like its fifteenth-century predecessors, it was clinker built and probably double-ended. It also had similar dimensions to the Blackfriars III barge (*Marsden, 1958: 129–134*).

There were also barges and other craft that combined the two techniques with strong flat bottoms and clinker sides. This combination of the two forms persisted in some types of sailing barge right into the nineteenth century. Most of the evidence for these craft was either from paintings or photographs. However, in recent years the surveys of the remains of a group of Humber keels on the former bed of the River Aire near Methley, and those of an Upper Severn trow at Lydney, have added to our knowledge. These are considered in more detail in later chapters. Frame-first carvel construction was a late arrival, and was probably in use in England by the late fifteenth century. The 'skeleton' of the ship or barge, the 'back bone' of a keel, a keelson, stem and stern posts and ribs or frames defining the shape of the hull, were erected first and then clad with a double skin of carvel planking. This technique became the norm for many vessels over the next four centuries until around 1870, when industrial iron shipbuilding largely replaced it. Smaller vessels such as barges continued to be built in wood. By the twentieth century many types of local barge had

Excavating the transom stern of a Mersey flat at Chester in 1998.

become extinct or were on the point of going out of service. In the 1930s, the Society for Nautical Research commissioned Philip Oke to record the lines and construction of many local types of wooden craft including sailing barges. Other individuals, such as Edgar March were inspired to do similar measuring and photographic work and to draw, write up and publish the results (*March, 1970*). The survey of other types of barges continued after the Second World War. For example, the measured surveys of abandoned hulks of Mersey flats by Frank Howard have provided more details about the construction and shape of their type (*Howard, 1999: 10–25*). The Society for Sailing Barge Research has also been assiduous in documenting the numerous abandoned hulks of Thames barges which existed around the creeks of the Thames estuary and the Essex rivers. Most of these archaeological relics have since been broken or buried. All these efforts have shown that, within any one type of barge, there are often detailed variations in terms of shape and construction, often according to the builder, the date and the place of building.

The record is incomplete even in 2007. No one, for example, has found the remains of a Tyne keel. In this case and others, different kinds of evidence have to be deployed, and quite often archaeological evidence alone is not enough to make sense of the remains of a barge. Other sources of evidence need to be used to gain a fuller understanding of how barges were built, sailed and employed. Water transport was crucial to the development of Britain, and especially its transformation from a rural to an industrial economy in the eighteenth and early nineteenth centuries. Barge development went hand in hand with this transformation, and one result of this is the availability of many more records and images.

It usually required an Act of Parliament to raise the funds, to make navigable and to charge dues on a river. There were an increasing number of Acts passed from the sixteenth century onwards to open uprivers for navigation. Some contain clauses which specify the kind of craft

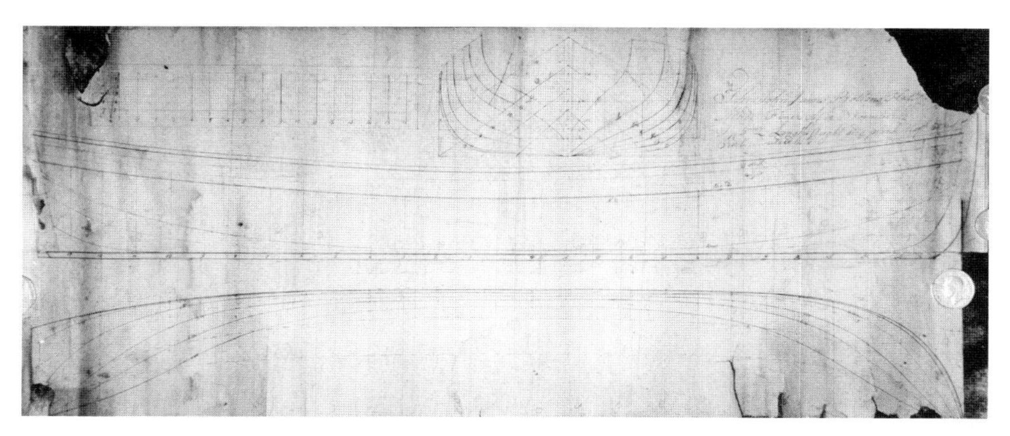

This manuscript plan of John James Bolton's flat dated 12 November 1782 is a rare example of an eighteenth-century plan of a sailing barge. (Photo by Mike Clarke, original in a private collection)

that might use the waterway. For example, there was an Act signed by Henry VIII in 1537 to authorise the removal of weirs and other impediments to navigation on the Irish river Barrow. One of its clauses referred to 'boats, scowtes, wherries, clarans, cottes and other vessels.' You can guess that some of these were cargo barges and others passenger or fishing vessels. A scowte might have been similar to the shoute – a small medieval barge on the Thames – and a wherry might have been a passenger rowing skiff, again like the wherries on the Thames. As for clarans, I pass. Cottes was an Irish word for a dug-out. It was also applied for the late nineteenth century trading barges on the Barrow and the neighbouring Suir and Slaney. A statutory register of British ships was established in 1786 and was organised by the local Custom Houses round the country. Sailing barges were included if they were coastal-going. Each registry entry contained the dimensions and rig of the barge and details of all the owners. Other records, such as surveys of inland barges in 1795 and 1798 and the census returns from 1841, are among the official records which provide other sources for details of individual barges and bargemen.

Non-official records of individual barges also survive, though not in huge numbers. For example, the records of the Gwydir estate on the River Conwy in North Wales contain the accounts for the building of a sailing barge (*Williams, 1980: 5–15*). In the same vein, Lancashire Record Office contains a detailed specification of the flat *Concorde* built at Wigan in 1742 (*Stammers, 1993: 20*). Most types of barge were built without using plans. Their builders relied on inherited experience and possibly half-models. So, plans such as that of James Bolton's 'flatte' of 1782 are rare indeed. Given the lack of statistics that measure barge traffic from coasters or narrow boats, sources such as trade directories and newspapers can provide useful indications of increasing trade through the lists of operators or regular carrying services. As early as 1684, Richard Vicars of the trow was running a cyclical service between Tewkesbury and Bristol and was to be found 'upon the key atte Bristol every springe tide' (*Hussey, 2000: 199*). Although to modern standards this does not appear to have been a particularly speedy service, Richard Vicar's roughly once a month deliveries would have been satisfactory in a less frenetic century than our own.

There is also a wealth of secondary sources. Sailing barges attracted an increasing interest from maritime historians and enthusiasts from the beginning of the twentieth century. This

Many pictures of barges were incidental to the main subject. In this case, it is the picturesque hump-backed Ouse Bridge at York in the eighteenth century. The artist has drawn the wrong kind of barge – it should be a keel and has got the rig back-to-front.

was at a time when sailing barges were beginning to become rare vessels. Magazines such as *Yachting Monthly* published pictures and plans of them. *The Mariner's Mirror* (the journal of the Society for Nautical Research established in 1910) published scholarly articles on different types of barge. The late Frank Carr's *Sailing Barges* which was first published in 1931 and went through second and third editions in 1951 and 1970 was one of the landmarks in this age of increased interest. Although many of its chapters were devoted to Thames barges, it did also cover the other main types of sailing barge. As can be seen in the bibliography, the number and range of publications which include sailing barges has become immense. They range from technical studies of individual types, to excavation reports, to reminiscences of retired barge skippers and monographs and articles on the economics of inland and coastal trading.

Pictures can provide evidence of the appearance and particularly the changing rigs of different types of barge. Medieval and older barges were either square or lug rigged. From the late sixteenth century there is increasing evidence of the use of fore and aft sails, including the gaff rig with a gaff and boom to support the main sail which pivot on the aft side of the mast. The standing gaff, one that is left aloft without a boom, and the spritsail, with a diagonal spar supporting the sail, were important variations. The triangular foresail, which was set between the stem and the mast on the forestay was vital in assisting a barge to tack. Being right forward in the bow, it exerted a large amount of leverage to shift the barges' bow through the wind and on to a new tack. This was not necessary for all barges, particularly ones on inland rivers – here the sails were really of use with the wind aft, otherwise they relied on towing by horses or teams of men. It is also important to remember than most

The contemporary scale model of the Mersey flat *Wesley* provides a lot of detailed information about its rig and deck layout. (Photo by Mike Clarke, model in private collection)

estuary barges relied on the power of the tides, and only worked with them rather than against them. Some barges, or rather lighters, that only had to move short distances between a moored ship and a quay could dispense with sails and rely on the tide and long oars known as sweeps.

Contemporary views of ports, either as backgrounds to portraits of ships or as topographic views, often included sailing barges. Most of the seventeenth-century ones are of London, which outstripped any other port for barge work and continued to do so until cargoes under sail were no longer carried. Wenceslaus Hollar's view of the Thames in 1647 showed great activity on the river with watermen working long sweeps to steer their sail-less lighters using the tide. There were also square-rigged barges carrying high stacks of hay or straw. These barges, unlike Blackfriars II, were swim-headed. They had flat-angled bows and sterns like punts. The accuracy of his barge pictures can be checked against other artists' views of the capital, such as that of Ogilby and Morgan of 1677. Samuel and Nathaniel

Such records can be interpreted in scale models such as this fine model of the *Daresbury* which was based on the plan and measurements from the sunken remains of the original flat. (The Boat Museum, Ellesmere Port)

Buck's engravings of London in 1749 continued to show these kinds of lighter along with other types of barge. The Bucks are important for sailing barge spotting because between 1728 and 1749 they produced waterfront views of forty other towns and cities with barges in the foreground. In this way, they give us a snapshot of barging activity around England and Wales in the early eighteenth century, just when the national economy was beginning to increase its rate of growth, and at a time when there was no cheaper, safer or faster alternative to water transport.

Pictorial evidence can be misleading. Artists could misunderstand the appearance of a barge; for example, the barge pictured at Ouse bridge, York, in a late eighteenth-century issue of *The Lady's Magazine* has a standing gaff main sail the wrong way round. The Bucks on the other hand did not make such mistakes, and their barges can also be checked against other pictures.

For example, the barges in their view of Newcastle were undoubtedly Tyne keels. Their Severn trows at Gloucester or Worcester look like trows. They also show how common it was to deploy square sails. Their views of inland towns such as Oxford, Ely or Burton-on-Trent all contained barges moving under a single square sail. They also show how the profile of some types of barge changed. For example, their Mersey flats and Thames barges were shorter with much more sheer than their successors.

Contemporary models of sailing barges are rare, but those that survive can be truly valuable sources for understanding their construction or rig. For example, no wrecks or buried remains of a Tyne keel have been discovered to date. This lack of such evidence makes the models of keels in the Newcastle Discovery Museum an invaluable source. In the same way, the rigged model of the sailing flat *Wesley* was a great help in understanding how lowering the mast on a flat was carried out. Models can also help interpret the plans and results of surveys of hulks and archaeological excavations. The shattered sunken remains of the oldest Mersey flat, the *Daresbury* of 1772, make little sense to the layman, but the scale model at the Boat Museum, Ellesmere Port, which was based on a measured survey, provides an insight into the hull design and rig of this unique sailing barge.

2

SAILING BARGES: THE INDUSTRIAL REVOLUTION AND AFTER

During the eighteenth and early part of the nineteenth centuries Britain underwent an acceleration of industrial and agricultural production and a rapid growth in population. These changes were accompanied by new industrial technologies – most notably the employment of steam engines – and improvements in the transport infrastructure. They transformed a predominantly rural economy into the first industrial one, which by 1850 had made Britain 'the workshop of the world'. This era has become known by the shorthand title of the 'Industrial Revolution'. Its origins, progress, landmarks and results continue to be a matter of debate.

Sailing barges had a role to play in this 'revolution'. This was because they, along with narrow boats and coasters, provided low-cost water transport for fuel, food, raw materials, building materials and many other commodities. For example, the Shropshire iron trade depended on the Severn, in spite of its navigational problems, to carry their manufactures down to Gloucester and Bristol. Newcastle was another example; the North-Eastern collieries were increasing their output to meet the rising demand for coal from homes and industries all the way down the East Coast and especially from London. While it is impossible to ascertain the volume of sailing barge traffic, it was closely linked to the thriving coastal trade. In 1768, *Baldwin's London Directory* listed 580 places to which goods could be sent by water (*Armstrong and Bagwell, 1983: 143*). The total tonnage of ships in the coastal trade rose from 154,640 tons in 1760 to 829,238 tons by 1830 (*Armstrong & Bagwell, 1983: 145*). The leading ports in the coastal trade used barges to collect and distribute cargoes inland. For example, Hull used keels to deliver to much of inland Yorkshire and Lincolnshire, while King's Lynn had the same role for west Norfolk and the counties of Cambridge and Huntingdon.

In this changing era, some kinds of sailing barge were transformed. They were built to larger tonnages and greater seaworthiness, so that they became flat-bottomed coasters, and were no longer confined to estuaries and inland waterways. On the other hand, like many other aspects of the Industrial Revolution, such changes were patchy. Some types of barge – most notably the Tyne keels – remained much as they were before, because by legislation, tradition or size, they remained suitable for their specific jobs. Changes in sailing barge design

Sailing barges were an essential component of the transport system which assisted the British Industrial Revolution. In major estuaries such as the Humber, sailing barges were built in their hundreds. (H. Carlidge/Humber Keel and Sloop Preservation Society)

were driven by economic considerations. They carried low-paying bulk freight, and the simpler and cheaper their build and rig combined with the smallest possible crew and the largest possible cargo capacity, the bigger the profit for their owners. Their design was also influenced by their natural environment, and by man-made features such as the depth of water in a canal or the dimensions of locks. Outside influences probably played their part. For example, the Scandinavian traditions of clinker building influenced the design of the clinker-built Norfolk wherry, while the Dutch, who were the dominant mercantile power for most of the seventeenth century, pioneered such important sailing barge features such as gaff and sprit rig, and leeboards. On the other hand, most barges were built in small and often isolated boat-building firms which passed first-hand experience down the generations and tended to stick with what had worked in the past, or what the owners would pay for.

The picture is complicated further by the sheer randomness of commercial life. Local types of barges moved out of their original operational area. Barges were changed and rebuilt after launching – trial and error in working could bring about improvements – and in any case no two barges were ever exactly the same. Some of these changes might have been incorporated in new boats or they might not. Older designs might operate alongside newer ones so long as there was work for them and they were in a repairable condition. Barges were transport vehicles whose owners ran them to make a profit or to deliver supplies to their main enterprises. With few exceptions, barges were built as cargo carriers, pure and simple. An example of an exception was the Thames barges, which were designed specifically to compete in the late nineteenth-century Thames and Medway barge races. For example, there was no point for a Humber barge owner converting his keel to sloop rig just because it was the latest thing. That was unless he was thinking of entering his keel into the outer estuary and coasting trade. The keel's square sails required less rigging and smaller spars. They were cheaper to buy and maintain than the gaff main sail and foresail of a sloop and their attendant standing and running rigging. Their lightness and simplicity was a positive advantage when the time came

Railways took much cargo away from sailing barges in the nineteenth century. Nevertheless sailing barges such as these Norfolk wherries at Great Yarmouth were able to earn a living up to about 1900. (Bob Malster)

to remove them temporarily to complete an inland delivery. Humber keel skippers were also adept at exploiting their square sails. They were not just running sails. Used with experience and skill, they were akin to a lugsail and could act on all points of sailing.

Hull cross-sections might differ, but the proportion of length to beam tended to be close among the different types of barge. The larger barges tended to have a beam to length ratio of around 1:4. The leanest was the River Arun barge which, at 58ft long and 10ft beam, had a ratio of 1:5.8. The chubbiest was the Tyne keel with a length of 42ft and breadth 21, which gave it a ratio of 1:2.1. Other smaller barges, such as those from the Solent, the Teign, the Fal and the Rother, all came in between 1:3.23 and 1:3.4. The size of locks was another important factor governing dimensions. Barges were built to fit the maximum dimensions of local locks and this included their draft. Coastal-going barges tended to be not so restricted especially in their drafts. All sailing barges had some sort of sheer, however minimal, and those that went coastwise had more than those that were confined to inland waters. Most barges were carvel built by the eighteenth century. Again, there were exceptions, such as the Norfolk wherries, where all the wooden ones were clinker built with one unique carvel-built exception. Then there were other barges, such as the upriver trows and the older Humber keels, which were built with a combination of clinker and carvel.

The most common sail was the single square sail. Often this sail was no more than something that was set only when the wind was fair, and was often used in combination with

Sailing barges – with their shallow draught and lowering masts – could carry cargoes well inland. Here, a group of clinker-built Humber keels were tied up at Doncaster almost 70 miles from Hull.

towing by horses or a team of haulers, or with the large oars known as sweeps. Sometimes the sail served for part of a voyage. On the Upper Bann and the Lagan Navigation, barges that had to cross Lough Neagh to reach the coal mines at Coalisland rigged temporary sails to carry them across the broad stretch of water. Mersey dumb flats that were normally towed might rig up a temporary sail from a hatch tarpaulin and a ladder. Gaff rig on a single mast was also a popular choice. Sometimes this was with a boom, as in the case of the Humber sloop, or boom-less, as in the case of the Norfolk wherry. The other main rig was the spritsail where a long diagonal spare supported the peak of the sail. This was useful in small craft because it could be easily unshipped. In larger vessels, the sprit was permanently rigged and the sail kept aloft, and was furled quickly by a series of ropes called brails. The lug rig was also found on the barges of the Rother and there were other variations such as barges fitted with bowsprits, which in turn might be fixed, lifting or sliding. Gaff rigged barges might carry temporary square sails for running, and big barges might be rigged as ketches, schooners and galliots. The latter two were very much in the minority.

Most barges had a single hold with crew accommodation and stores in the bow and the stern. It is likely that most of the older barges, whatever their type, had open holds. The large coastal trows built in the late nineteenth century continued the practice of open holds protected by canvas side cloths. Barges on tidal waters would have some kind of windlass to heave up an anchor, and over time the larger barges added multi-sheave tackles and special winches to raise the sails and leeboards. These allowed the crew, who usually numbered no more than two or three, to work larger vessels.

The dominance of water transport, which had been reinforced by the piecemeal construction of a network of inland narrow canals in the late eighteenth century, was

Upriver ports such as Colchester were largely served by sailing barges in spite of the narrowness of the River Colne. Round about 1930, the *Imperial* and another barge were tied up to the left, while an empty barge is being winched downstream.

challenged by the arrival of railways with steam locomotives. The Stockton and Darlington Railway opened in 1825 and cut out a large amount of coal lighterage on the River Tees because it delivered coal in trucks directly to coasters. The Liverpool and Manchester Railway which opened in 1830 was in direct competition with the flats plying on the Mersey & Irwell Navigation and the Bridgewater Canal. The flats held their own with the increasing assistance of steam tugs for another decade before the railway took a dominant position. The Liverpool and Manchester was the pioneer of long-distance steam railways and within twenty years of its opening there was a national network of lines. So, for example, it became possible to carry coal in trucks direct from the mines of the North-East to London. Nevertheless, Britain's industrial growth meant that there was still plenty of cargo for sailing barges.

After 1850, the British economy's rate of growth began to slow, and by 1900 it was suffering the effects of competition from other nations, especially Germany and the United States. Railways continued to be built. Local branch lines continued to be opened and often took away traffic from sailing barges, while agriculture, which had provided many barge cargoes, became increasingly depressed by competition with cheaper imports of grain and meat. The picture across the estuaries was uneven. Tyne keels were in terminal decline by the 1860s, as were the barges of the Sussex rivers and the Upper Severn trows. Most Mersey sailing flats had been turned into dumb barges by 1900, leaving the sailors with the coal bunkering, sand and coastal trades. The Lower Severn and Bristol Channel were probably worked by around 100 trows in the latter part of the nineteenth century, and there were an estimated 2,000 Thames sailing barges working in 1900.

Numbers of barges working under sail declined rapidly in the early twentieth century. The most critical factor was the lack of replacements for the tired and worn out older barges. Very few sailing barges were launched after 1900. In the case of the Severn trow and the Mersey flat

Many dumb barges were modelled on the lines of the earlier sailing flats. This new dumb flat was launched at Runcorn about 1900. (W. Leathwood)

the last launches were in 1906, the last trading wherry went down the ways in 1912, and the last Thames barge in 1930. And it was not just competition from the railways; large numbers of motor lorries came on to the market at the end of the First World War. Although they had limited range at first, in the long-term they were to become the predominant method of bulk transport. The other threat, which also applied to British-owned steam coasters, was from the large fleet of new, efficient diesel coasters built up by Dutch owners. They competed for many barge freights, particularly on the East Coast.

The biggest fleet remained the Thames barges, but most other types of barge had been reduced to single numbers under sail. More survived as dumb or motor barges. For example, there was a good selection of former trows in the Lydney coal trade after the Second World War, and motorised Norfolk wherries found work carrying dredgings and also sugar beet in to the factory at Cantley during the autumn and winter. Many keels worked under motor during the same era because there was a thriving lighterage trade between Hull and upriver factories, as well as large tonnages of coal to be shifted from the mines of south Yorkshire. Many Thames barges were equipped with auxiliary engines, and then gradually reduced in rig. The mizzen was the first to go, followed by the top sail. A motor barge would have no more than a light mast to carry a navigation light and no sails. It simply was not worth finding replacements to sails and spars once they had worn out. Most of the motor and auxiliary barges worked up to the early 1960s. By 1963, only one barge, the *Cambria*, continued to carry cargo under sail alone. In 1966, she was sold by her original owners, F.T. Everard, to her skipper, who continued in trade for another four years. Apart from being worn out through old age, barges had too small a cargo capacity; many of their old customers such as coal merchants and millers had gone out of business, and there was an ever-increasing volume of long-distance road haulage which could deliver door-to-door.

Some new barges, such as the dumb flat *Monkey Brand* of 1900, were built along traditional lines but in steel instead of wood. There were many steel-hulled Thames barges. (National Museums Liverpool)

Nostalgia for barges would have been hard to credit in the nineteenth century, and this was because they were hard-worked and largely unadorned vessels with little romance about them, particularly when compared with the stately battleship of the line or the dashing tea clipper. All the same, as they disappeared through competition from railways and steam-powered coasters, their passing was regretted. Perhaps the earliest expression of regret was Charles Lamb's essay on 'The old *Margate Hoy*' which was published around 1820. He wrote: 'Can I forget thee, thou old *Margate Hoy*, with thy old weather-beaten, sun-burnt captain, and his rough accommodations – ill exchanged for the foppery and fresh-water niceness of the modern steam-packet?' Regret at the loss of other traditional craft began to find a voice in the early twentieth century. As mentioned in Chapter One, traditional sailing barges and fishing boats began to generate interest among local and maritime historians. Articles were published, photographs taken, reminiscences recorded and hulls measured and drawn. Museums that dealt with maritime collections also began to take notice. The Science Museum took the lead, and the new National Maritime Museum (founded in 1934 with a largely naval mission) followed, as did major provincial port museums such as those at Liverpool and Hull. Part of their collecting was devoted to finding contemporary models and part to commissioning new models to fill any gaps in their coverage. There was no thought of preserving full-size vessels, although there were a few privately owned Thames barges and Norfolk wherries sailing as yachts.

After the Second World War the first sailing barge preservation societies were set up to save the full-size article. The Thames Barge Sailing Club was set up in 1948 and was followed by the Norfolk Wherry Trust in 1949. The TBSC chartered and owned a number of barges before settling for the *Centaur* (1895) and the *Pudge* (1922). It set out to allow its members to enjoy barge sailing and to perpetuate the skills of the sailing barge skippers. In the early

Many sailing barges lost their sails and were towed or provided with diesel engines. The boomie *Thalatta* of 1906 was working as a motor barge at Ipswich in 1963.

years, it was able to recruit retired bargemen, but latterly as these old hands passed on, they trained their own volunteers to take command. Many more Thames barges have been preserved by individual owners and associations for youth work etc. Many find work as charter barges, where they hire themselves out for holidays, day trips, or corporate hospitality. There are about twenty-five active Thames barges at present, but the number always fluctuates as some are rebuilt and others are downgraded to static use or broken up.

Sailing barge preservation organisations were established to save other types of barge. The Humber Keel and Sloop Preservation Society was set up in the 1975, and acquired and re-rigged the keel *Comrade* (1923) and later undertook the restoration of the sloop *Amy Howson* (1914). By then, their options for preserving a keel and sloop were limited to steel hulls. To an extent, this has saved the society from some of the huge costs of maintaining old wooden hulls. Most wooden barges that are still sailing have had to undergo major rebuilding, and at present the *Pudge* is undergoing a partial reconstruction which will cost £160,000. The right quality and size of timber, the scarcity of shipyards with experienced labour, not to mention

Most sailing barges worked with a crew of two. In the case of the flat *Mayfly,* it was an old man and a lad. (D. Cross)

all the costs of maintaining sails and rigging, plus running costs such as insurance, make maintaining a sailing barge a job needing huge effort and dedication.

Alternatives to keeping an old barge sailing include preservation and display ashore or building a replica. There is huge disagreement among preservationists (of barges and other sorts of craft) as to whether it is more important to conserve as much of the original structure as possible or whether it is better to keep the barge sailing, which necessitates replacing large amounts of the original vessel. There is no definitive answer to these opposed positions, but one cannot help thinking that the conservation school makes too much of a mantra about preserving the original structure. Most older barges are rebuilds, and in any case any timbers that are replaced can be recorded. Static vessels displayed afloat or out in the open eventually succumb to neglect, and there is quite a history of museums acquiring barges and other vessels in a fit of enthusiasm, and then not having the running costs to pay for their proper maintenance. The continuing neglect of canal barges includes the last example of a Mersey flat at the Boat Museum at Ellesmere Port. The under cover static preservation of the *Spry*, the last Severn trow at Blist's Hill, Ironbridge, is justified

Work on sailing barges was always hard. Some barges like the Thames version had winches to assist the crew in handling the sails.

because she is unique and the costs of maintaining her afloat were beyond the museum. Also, the Severn is still a difficult river in which handle such a big and precious vessel. She undertook a number of demonstration sails after her restoration, and these have been recorded on film. Replicas are another possibility of putting back extinct barges back on their former waterways. There are quite a number of European replicas of traditional barges. The most outstanding in the British Isles is the billyboy *Audrey*, which was built from the hull of a Humber estuary lightship. There are also two Thames barges – the *Alice* and the *Betula* – that have been built out of the hulls of a Thames swim-headed lighter and a Dutch motor barge. The future may see other replicas built as the older barges are retired and I look forward to the possibility of seeing a Mersey flat under sail for the first time in over sixty years!

Although this work concentrates on summarising the history and characteristics of as many of the local sailing barges for which information exists, we should not forget the work and life of the bargemen. The detailed knowledge of their own waters was crucial to these professionals. Running aground too often (except for discharging or loading) would soon earn a skipper the

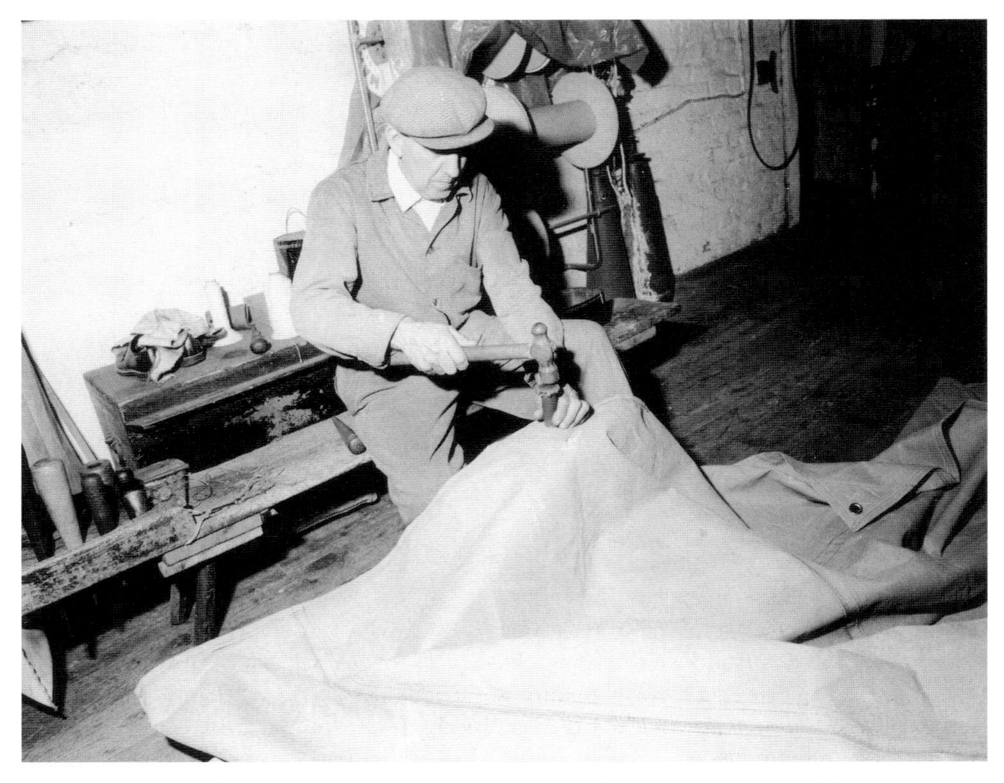

Maintaining sailing barges requires expensive and scarce skill such as sail making. (National Museums Liverpool)

sack, and navigating most estuaries and coastal waters was not straightforward because of the numerous shoals, sand banks, currents or rocks. Yet dangerous waters such as the Thames estuary or the Bristol Channel were sailed year in, year out by these hardy skippers with their minimal crews. It called for long hours round the clock, because barges invariably had to work with the tides. Equally, they had to be ready to load and discharge when ordered. Most bargemen did not own their vessels. But for all these features of a hard life, bargemen enjoyed a greater independence than in a job ashore. The wages were higher than those offered to land workers, even though they were generally paid as a proportion of the earnings on the freight. So: no cargo, no wages. They also had the advantage over the deep-sea merchant seaman, in that their voyages were normally short and that they had the comfort of a home and family ashore between trips. There were also distinct districts or villages where barge families held sway and these often contained barge building and repair yards as well. The hamlet of Pin Mill on the River Orwell is a good rural example, while the most distinctive (and long-vanished) urban bargemens' community was undoubtedly the Tyne keelmen's district of Sandgate in Newcastle-upon-Tyne.

These first two chapters have concentrated on the archaeology and history of sailing barges in a broad way. Yet most sailing barges were locally based and the best way to proceed is on a region by region basis, starting in the North-East of England (for no special reason), and going round the coast to finish in the North-West, with a final chapter for the Celtic nations of Wales, Scotland and Ireland.

3

THE KEELS AND WHERRIES OF NORTH-EAST ENGLAND

Of all the different types of regional or local barge, the River Tyne keel is among the best known. It is commemorated in the famous folk song, *The Keel Row*, and remains a local icon in spite of disappearing well over a century ago. The keel carried coal from mines inland to seagoing vessels lying below the old medieval bridge at Newcastle or to ships lying at the mouth of the river at North or South Shields. The keel's operations were tightly regulated by ancient statutes which dated back to 1350 and the reign of Edward III. A group of businessmen known as the 'Coal Fitters' were in charge of the coal traffic. They were members of the Company of Hostmen at Newcastle, which was a medieval guild whose original function was to act as hosts and guarantors for visiting merchants seeking to buy coal. The Hostmen were granted a monopoly of coal handling by the Crown in return for an annual payment. Most of the early keels were owned by the Coal Fitters. Later on, some keels were owned by the keelmen themselves, but they were subject to binding contracts with the Fitters and could not trade on their own account until 1872.

Over the centuries, the capacity of the keel changed. It was measured in 'chaldrons', a local term for a wagon load and a measurement of volume. By 1635, a keel load had been settled at eight chaldrons which amounted to 21.2 tons in weight. All new keels were to be measured by the King's Commissioners by loading them with a set amount of coal. The new keel was then marked with a load line ('the stock nail mark'). This load line could not be legally exceeded by loading more coal into the keel to the extent of submerging that line (*Finch, 1973: 25*). However, there seems to have been plenty of latitude for sharp practice. The 'nail mark' was a measure of displacement and thus weight. Colliery owners were known to add extra coal on their chaldrons to avoid some of the coal tax which was levied per keel load, rather than on a chaldron. They could squeeze as much as an extra 2 tons on each keel. It meant that the keels were overloaded, and the keelman had a lot of extra casting (shovelling) for no extra money. They were only paid by the tide (i.e. for the trip down from the colliery to the ship and unloading the coal). Coasting vessels often had their cargo capacity quoted in keels rather than tons. Yet it was not until 1832 that the keel became recognised as a measurement of weight, and

The Buck's view of Newcastle of 1745 included many keels working on the Tyne. They include examples of the traditional keelmens' practice with three men labouring at a massive oar, a sculling/steering oar over the stern and a simple square sail.

it remained a standard measure of a coaster's capacity all along the East Coast until about the 1870s.

The keels were loaded through 'spouts' – gravity-fed hoppers from staiths or quays where the coal was stored (often under cover). The early nineteenth century saw the development of coal drops below Newcastle, where seagoing ships could take on their cargo directly. Chapman's patent coal drop of 1807 was the first of its kind and was followed in 1812–13 by Thompson's coal cranes, which tipped a whole wagonload of coal down a chute. From the 1820s these coal drops grew in number and sophistication. As they received their consignments, first by horse-drawn tramways and later by steam railway, they represented a threat to the keel's monopoly. Nevertheless, keels were still needed for the carriage from the upriver staiths above the bottleneck of the old Newcastle bridge. The shallowness of the Tyne below the bridge meant that many ships could only load part of their cargoes at the coal drops and had to top them off from keels while anchored at the mouth of the river (*Osler, 2006*).

The position of the keel and the antique conventions of its trade were gradually eroded by new technologies and organisations. The arrival of the steam tug in the 1830s offered a more reliable (though more expensive) method of moving keels than the tide and the wind. The establishment of the Tyne Improvement Commission in 1852 led to a programme of dredging and other improvements, which enabled larger vessels direct access to upriver without incurring the risk of stranding or delay. Steam colliers, which were introduced in the 1850s, loaded directly from staiths, and so did not require keels. The replacement of the old bridge by a swing bridge in 1876 and further dredging allowed seagoing ships to berth above Newcastle. All this meant that the end of the keel was in sight.

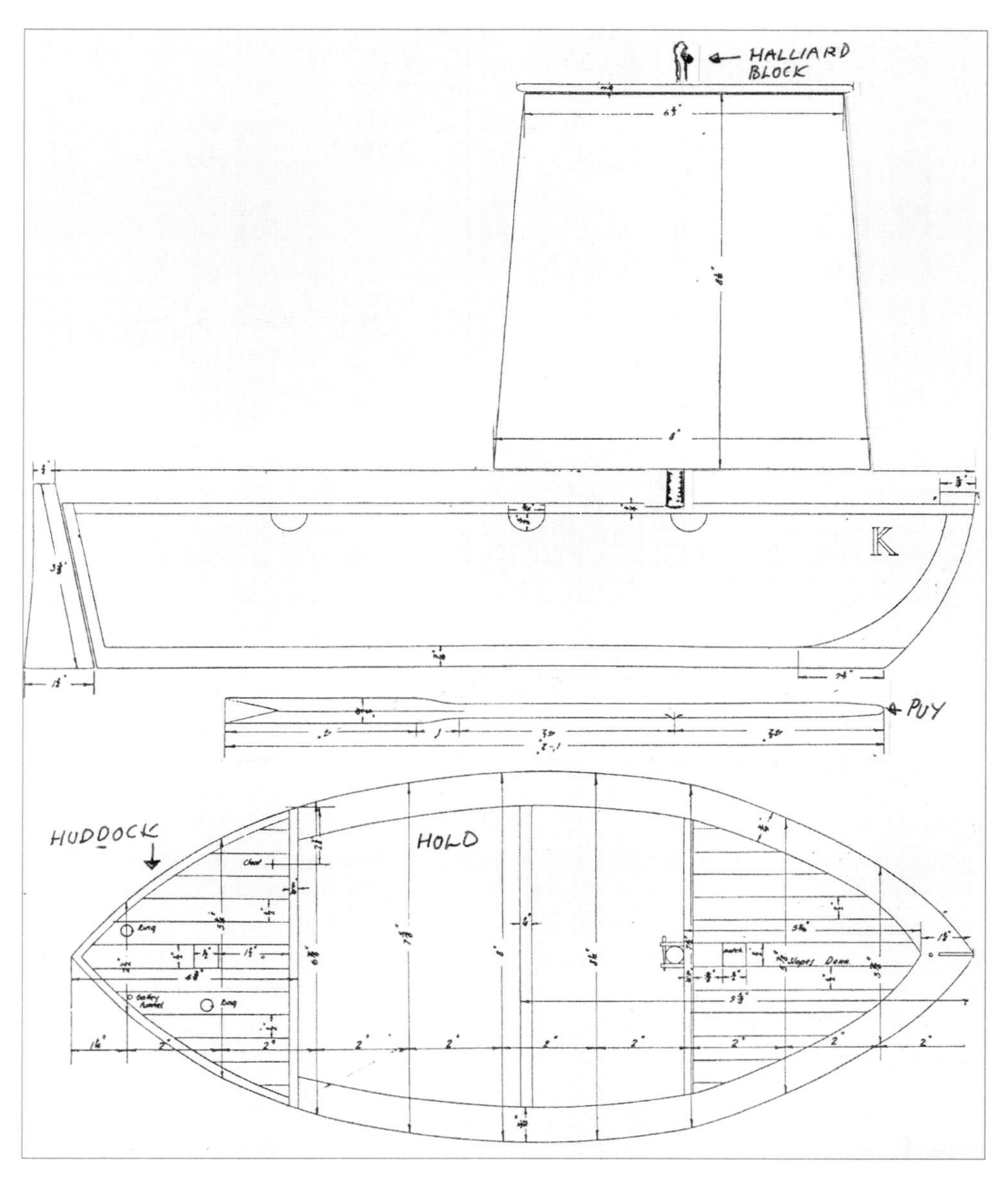

H.R.Viall's plan of the keel model *K*, now at Newcastle Discovery Museum, provides as accurate a set of dimensions as is possible given that no full-size keels survived to be recorded.

No one is sure how many keels there were at work in their heyday. It is generally agreed that there were about 300 at the time of the 1822 keelmen's strike. By 1827, the number was estimated to be 228, of which forty-three worked downriver from the bridge. In 1845, half the coal shipped from the Tyne was still being transhipped in keels. By the early 1860s, only a third of coal moved on the Tyne was handled in keels, although the total volume handled had increased. It has been estimated that there were about 250 craft working in river transport, and they included wherries and other barges as well as keels. Most of these

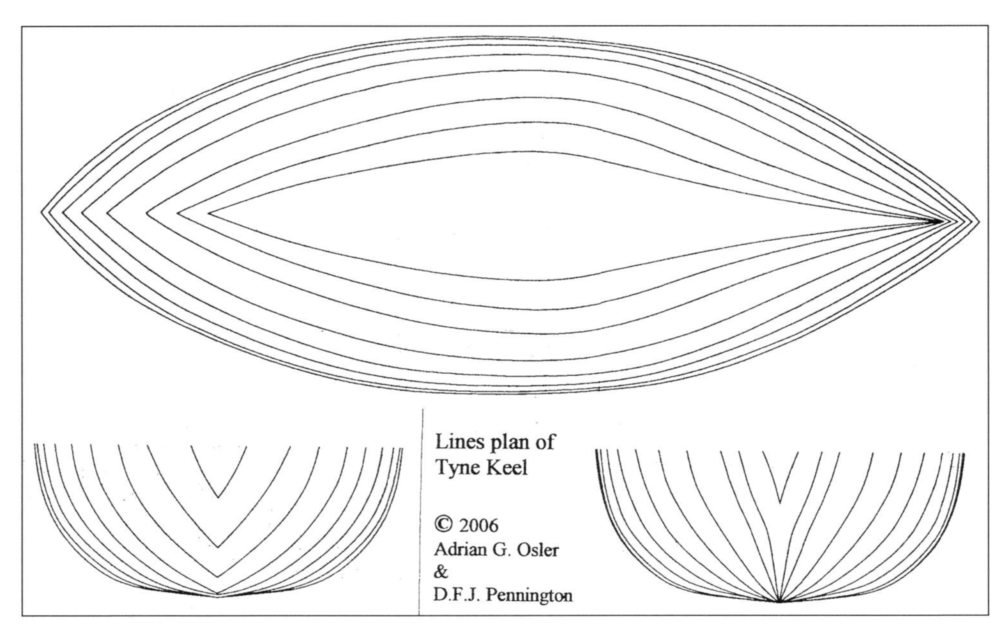

The same model has also been used to produce a line plan of a keel which showed that its hull form was well adapted for its trade. (Adrian G. Osler & D.F.J. Pennington)

Keels became one of the icons of Newcastle and the Tyne. They were depicted in many views of the nineteenth-century city. This shows the old fixed bridge before it was replaced in 1876. Several keels were piled high with coal. The crew of the one in the centre were raising its mast after shooting the bridge. This was sprit rigged, and the one to the right had rigged its light weather stunsail.

This print by J.W. Carmichael shows keels under sail at the mouth of the Tyne. It would appear that they were capable of reaching as well as running before the wind.

craft relied on steam towage. By the 1880s there was only one colliery operating the old upriver keels, and several more were used by downriver chemical factories. In 1893, it was reported that there were only six genuine keels left. A plea for one of these survivors to be preserved failed to gain any support (*Osler, 2006*). According to Finch: 'With their purpose gone many keels found honourable retirement employed as landing stages for the Tyne passenger steamers and a few found use with riverside industries as towed lighters' (*Finch, 1973: 30*).

Four models of keels survive in the Newcastle Discovery Museum, along with paintings and drawings of the Tyne in which they often supplied the foreground interest. So far, no one has disinterred the remains of a Tyne keel. Viall conducted an extensive search in the 1930s without success (*Viall, 1942: 161*). Combining all these indirect sources gives a reasonably accurate idea of the main features of the Tyne keel. The hull was strongly built with eight or nine broad oak or elm carvel strakes (planks) which were made from shorter pieces of wood. It was a tradition which is probably apocryphal that keels were built from the leftover materials of bigger ships. This carvel skin was fastened by treenails and copper spikes to substantial frames. The latter were closely spaced so that 'only a man's fist could go between them' (*Viall, 1942: 161*). The framing on the surviving Tyne wherry is witness to this practice. There was a large open hold amidships and short decks at the bow and stern. Within the main body of the hull there was a heavy platform amidships some 18in to 2ft below the sheer line. The 21.2-ton keel-load of coal was piled up to 6ft high on this, and retained by stout uprights (jells) and horizontal boards (deals). One side of the deals (the bye-side) could be removed for loading and unloading. In later keels, the hold platform might be extended

J.W. Carmichael also illustrated a keel being used to lighter large baulks of timber. Newcastle was the centre of the Baltic trade and imported large quantities of masts and spars.

towards the gunwale on the bye-side. This was to ease the keelmen's task of casting (shovelling) the coal either on to the ship's deck or through 18in by 12in coal ports in the sides of their hull (*Osler, 2006*).

Although the cargo capacity of the keel was laid down by statute, its exact dimensions are a matter of debate. The register of keels has been lost and the surviving models may not be precisely to scale. Reliable authors such as Viall agree on a 42ft length, but Osler has pointed out that the few keels that were recorded in the Custom House Shipping Registers had a length of 48ft. These latter records are considered reliable because they were documents of ownership. The keels listed in the Ship Registers must have been seagoing because there was no reason to register a river boat. There may have been two types of keel – one seagoing and one for river use only. The keel's beam has usually been estimated to be half its length. However, the models and the ship registers suggest that they had a narrower beam of 40–42 per cent of the length. This gives a beam of between 16.8 and 17.6ft for the shorter keel and 19 to 20ft for the longer one (*Osler, 2006*). This narrower beam would have assisted the keel's 'shallow-draughted, round-bottomed hull' form, whose low frictional and form resistance was ideal for its slow speed work. Keel builders, though, would have hardly understood such theory, but well appreciated the empirical result! Regrettably, we still know too little of the daily work of the men who built the keels and the ships they served – the shipwrights (*Osler and Barrow, 1993: 24*). Their depth was about 6ft with a draft of 4ft 6in. They had a curved stem and a straight stern post and no sheer.

At the stern there was a rudimentary cabin known as a 'huddock' for sheltering the crew which consisted of a skipper, two 'keel bullies' and the 'pee-dee' (a boy). The latter might stand in the huddock's hatchway to steer the vessel. A rudder was a late innovation. Keels were traditionally steered by a long steering and sculling oar known as a 'swape'. This was very much like the medieval barges on the Thames. It was also recorded in the Bucks' view of

Sailing keels above Newcastle bridge; note the early paddle tug – a sign of things to come.

Newcastle of 1745. Forward of the hold three of the crew worked a long oar in an iron rowlock to provide the main propulsion. These massive oars were apparently up to 22ft long and 7in in diameter. There were also two 30ft poles with forked ends known as 'puys', which were used to push the keel through the shallows. They were used up to depths of 18ft. Upriver, where the banks permitted it, keels might be towed by the crew when the other forms of propulsion would not work.

Keels carried a square sail to exploit the prevailing westerly winds when working down the Tyne while loaded. This was carried on a yard, usually about 15 to 18ft long on a 20ft mast. It contained about 240 sq. ft (or 50–60 yards) of canvas. It was hoisted by a halliard with a tie to the yard and tackle. The mast was housed in a triangular tabernacle and was supported by two shrouds and a forestay. These could be released as the mast and sail were lowered by the crew when shooting the low arches of the bridge at Newcastle. Contemporaries considered that keels could be sailed close to the wind and tacked smartly. This may be correct because keelmen were known to keep the luff of the sail tight by two bowlines. They could also sling the yard like a lugsail, which would have contributed to their handiness. Some keels had an extended cutwater (stem) which would have also helped their lateral resistance. The sail could be reefed in high winds and extended by an extra sail (stunsail) set on a temporary bowsprit in light weather (*Osler, 2006*).

The old style of keel operation became increasingly difficult to sustain by the 1830s and '40s. As a result some keels were converted for local seagoing work with a fore-and-aft rig of a sprit main sail (known as a 'spreat' locally) and a foresail. With about 82 yards of canvas, this was a comparatively expensive rig. The conservative upriver operators felt obliged to follow suit and, by 1838, the square sail was becoming a rarity. The spreat rig in turn gradually gave way

The Keelmens' Hospital with a procession of keelmen in their 'Sunday best'.

to the power of the steam paddle tugs which could tow a string of eight keels whatever the wind or the tide. Thus, by the 1860s sailing keels were few and far between.

In the 1820s, just before the beginning of their decline, it was estimated that keels provided employment for 850 keelmen (*Rowe, 1973*). Perhaps a sign of incipient decline was the decision after the end of the 1822 strike not to recruit any more boys. The keelmen formed an old, distinctive, close-knit and sometimes disruptive community in the Sandgate area of the city. They were visually distinctive from the rest of the waterfront workers both in their everyday dress and their Sunday best. The former usually consisted of a short jacket, waistcoat and knee breeches in flannel (usually grubby with coal dust), bright blue stockings, dark blue shirt with red neckerchief and a blue bonnet with a red top bobble similar to the Scots' tam-o'-shanter. The off-duty dress was even more flamboyant, with a spotless white shirt with a red or black silk neckerchief, a yellow waistcoat, a blue jacket, slate-coloured bell-bottom trousers and a black silk hat tied with a long ribbon which streamed out behind the wearer (*Osler, 1984: 74–75*). The latter seemed to have been in imitation of naval costume of the early nineteenth century. Nevertheless, locally, it was a badge of the keelmen's separateness and was probably unique among the all the sailing bargemen elsewhere. The latter were to some extent separated from land communities because of their calling, but did not dress in a way that distinguished them from other seafarers and waterfront workers. The Keelmen's Hospital in City Road which was erected in 1701 is another witness to the separateness of the keelmen. The building is still standing and has been turned into student accommodation, where doubtless the keelmen's traditions of hard drinking are perpetuated.

At the same time as the keels declined, there was a growing need for larger general-purpose barges to carry both raw materials and finished goods along the river, and lighter goods to

The *Elswick No.2* is the last of the Tyne wherries and, drawn up out of the water, shows off its graceful underwater shape. (Tyne and Wear Museum's Service)

and from ships. These new barges were known as wherries. Their builders resorted to the clinker building method. This was simple, expeditious and economical, and had been practised in Northumbria since the days of the first Anglo-Saxon and Viking settlers. It was also used for the paddle tugs that were being built in increasing numbers on the Tyne, not only for local use but for havens all down the East Coast. The wherry was constructed of an outer shell of overlapping planks using only one template amidships to get the shape correct. Once fastened together, the heavy strengthening internal frames and deck beams were inserted. A wherry had to be strongly built to resist being crushed against other ships in the docks and to withstand regular groundings at low tide.

The early wherries seem to have been quite small and it is possible, although not proven, that they developed from smaller passenger ferries, possibly similar to the Thames wherries. The name was certainly in use by the 1820s and was eventually transferred to the larger later lighters. In 1824 they were reported to be 31ft 6in long, 11ft beam and 3ft draught and carrying 7 tons (*Osler, 2006*). Certainly the painting of the Tyne with a wherry that was auctioned at Sotheby's in 1983 showed a small barge. This picture also showed that, like the Norfolk wherry, this Tyne wherry had a quarter round white patch painted on its bow. Could that suggest another origin? Early nineteenth-century Norfolk wherries were small in comparison with later versions and had been known to operate outside of their native area, as did, for example, the eight that sailed to Portsmouth harbour in 1857 (*Clark, 1961: 138–142*).

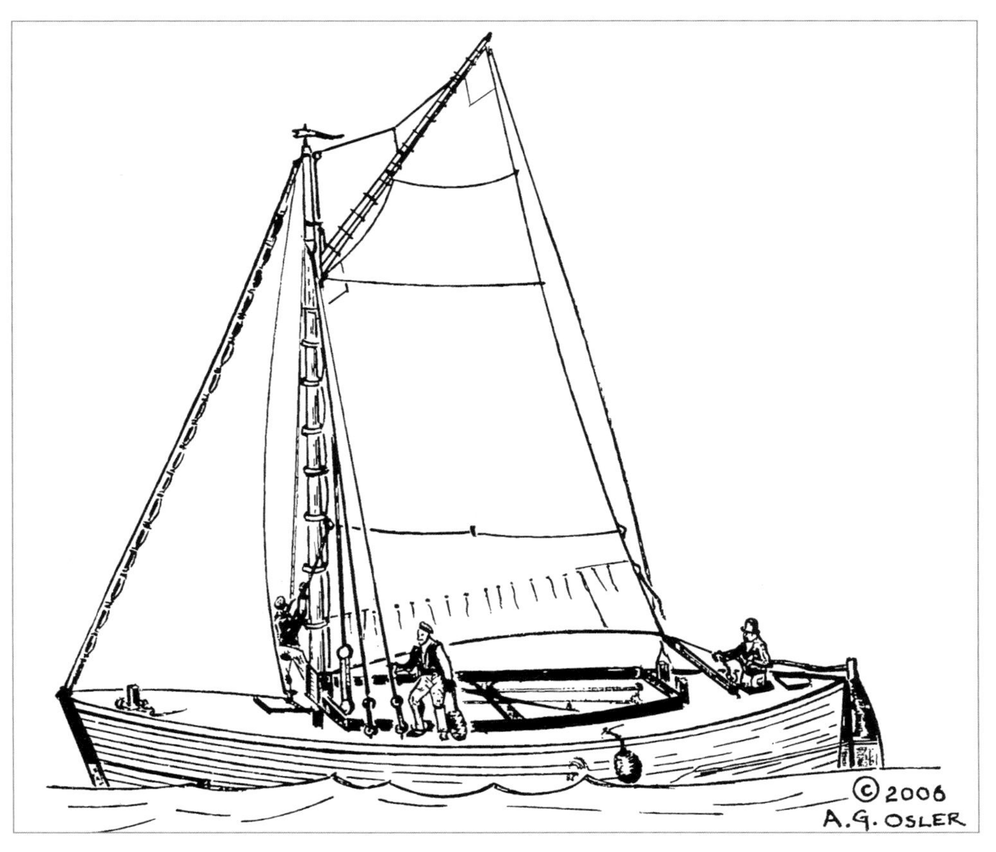

The Tyne wherry *Jane* by Adrian Osler from a painting by John Scott, 1850. Sailing close-hauled under a main sail rigged on a standing gaff. Note the three brails to furl the sail and the vangs which control the end of the gaff. She had been registered at South Shields and had a tonnage of 26 tons. She doubtless undertook coastal deliveries as well as river work. (Adrian G. Osler)

Later wherries tended to be about 50ft long and 20ft in the beam and could carry 35–40 tons of cargo. Wherries were propelled in the same fashion as the keels, and had either a main sail with a standing gaff and no boom or a spritsail. Either rig could be easily stowed aloft using brails. Wherries were mainly dumb and towed by the growing number of paddle tugs on the Tyne. In the later nineteenth century, many were built as self-propelled steam barges which were nicknamed 'puffers'. They were also fitted with a hand-operated deck crane.

The *Elswick No.2*, dating from 1931, is the only survivor of this type and was the last to be launched. She is nearly 55ft long with a 23ft beam – not dissimilar proportions to the keel. Her outer skin is made up from 1in-thick oak planks and her frames measure 5in by 6in and are closely spaced. Like many of her kind, she was designed as a dumb barge and was later fitted with a motor. She was owned by Vickers, the engineers who specialised in moving heavy pieces of machinery downriver for export. She was later owned by N. Keedy & Sons and used for ferrying prefabricated steel sections between different shipyards. In 1976, at the end of her working life, she was bought by the Maritime Trust for preservation, and later transferred to the Tyne and Wear Museums Service. She is on show at the regional Large Object Store at Beamish.

A Tees keel taking a consignment of wheat from a brig at Stockton around 1860. She has a short-raked mast right for a lug sail which is barely discernible against the ship's rigging. (Peter Barton)

The other rivers of the North East – the Blyth, the Wear and the Tees also had some sailing barges. They were described as keels and seem to have been built to similar proportions, although of larger dimensions than the Tyne keels. There is evidence for this from the remains of a lighter found by Viall on the River Blyth (*Viall, 1942: 161*). On the Wear, similar barges operated which were known as keels. Some were used for an early form of containerisation, transporting standardized coal tubs. As on the Tyne, the installation of coal-tipping equipment and linking railway lines made such barges obsolete. Nevertheless, the existence of quays and staiths on either bank as far up the Wear as Biddick, some 5 miles inland from Sunderland, prove the past existence of vibrant traffic carried in the local keels. Marwood's *Annual Directory, Shipping Register and Commercial Advertiser* of 1854 listed ten collieries which paid river duty, implying that they were still using water transport rather than the coal tips in the docks. His list of locally registered vessels included, among all the collier snows, thirty-three sloops which ranged from between 16 and 35 tons, and were (with a few exceptions) all locally built.

They included the *Black Adventure* and the *Thomas and Grace* which were both built at Newcastle and registered as 22 tons. They sound like keels that had been moved to the Wear. It is unclear whether these sloops were the local Wear barges; they are certainly not fishing vessels because Marwood only included cargo vessels. They may have served local coastal settlements which had no harbours. There were certainly other Wear barges which traded only within the river and would not have been recorded in the official Ship Registers, which were the source of Marwood's lists.

Stockton was the main port on the River Tees in the eighteenth century. It enjoyed a thriving trade in exporting agricultural produce and lead. Some of these cargoes were

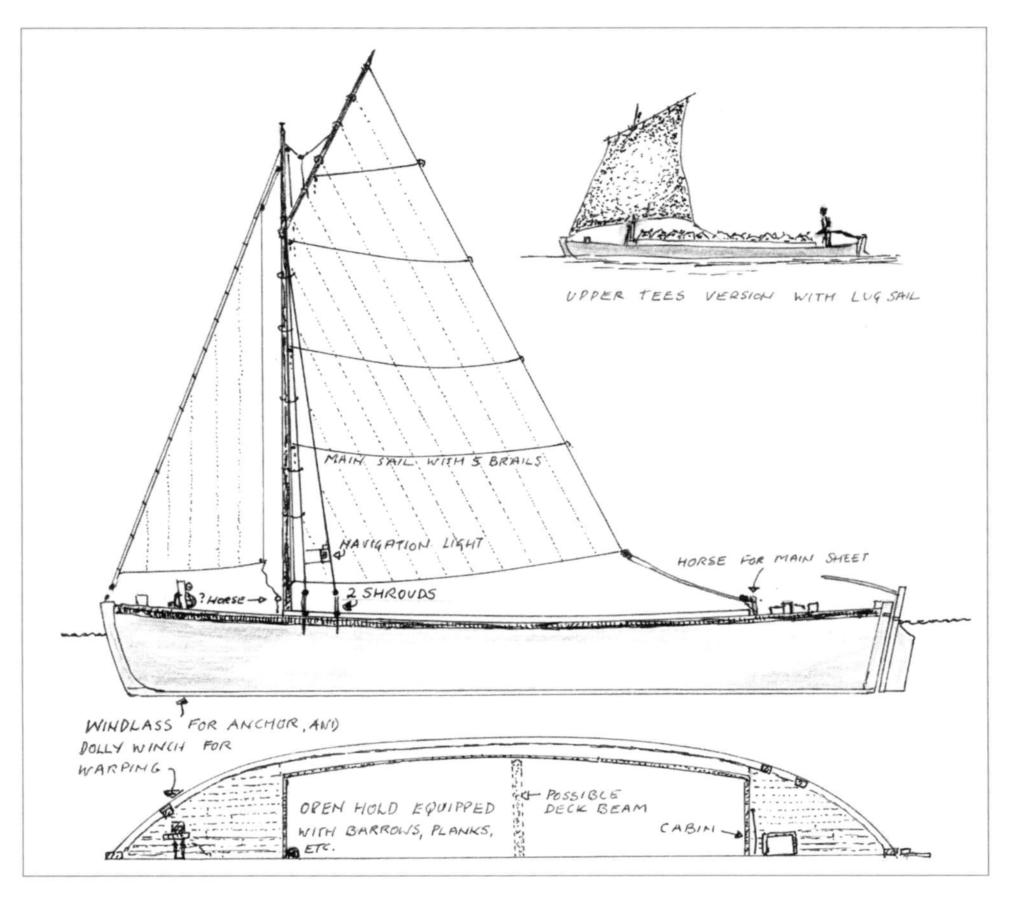

The sail plan and basic layout of a Tees sand wherry based on oral testimony and contemporary photographs.

brought down by barges from further up the Tees, especially from Yarm and the head of navigation at Low Worsall. In the eighteenth century, small craft carrying about 4 tons, called either boats or cobles, transported copper, iron, lead, agricultural produce, household and other goods down to Stockton. They were manned by five crew and equipped with a mast. There seems to have been a cessation of this trade in 1779 when the local Peirse family went bankrupt. The navigation rights were later leased to a group of merchants who had a particular interest in shipping lead. In 1801, they hired a Sunderland keel which could carry up to 57 tons of lead (when the depth of the river allowed it) to make the passage up to Low Worsall (*Barton, 2006*).

The shallows and shoals of the River Tees below Stockton meant that some vessels preferred to discharge in the lower reaches at places such as Coatham, and barges were probably then used to move the cargo up to Stockton. The middle of the nineteenth century saw a massive improvement in the conservancy of the Tees and the establishment of new ports in the lower reaches, with Middlesbrough and its chemical industries as the hub (*Barrow, 2005: 12–16*). All of this eclipsed Stockton and the upriver traffic. Barges seem to have continued to operate. Marwood listed four keels under the Stockton registry in 1854, including the *Despatch* of 37 tons, built at Yarm in 1816, and the *John & Laura* of 34 tons, built at Stockton in 1840.

Engravings from Yarm all the way downstream, and dating from the mid- to the late nineteenth century, show craft with either a square sail or sloop rigged. Two photographs of the quays at Stockton in the 1860s show large keel-like lighters assisting the unloading of seagoing ships. Both carried a small lugsail forward of the hold. They were double-ended, clinker-built vessels about 50ft long with an open hold. Two later nineteenth-century photographs of the Stockton waterfront and the Union Dock, Hartlepool, show large keel-like lighters without sails but with the coal-loading decks that were fitted in the Tyne keels.

Peter Barton, who is the authority on the maritime history of the Tees, had the good fortune to interview Tom Buckton, who had been born in 1884 and worked on the sand wherries. These were used for collecting sand either at the mouth of the Tees or, if freshwater sand or gravel were required, upriver as far as Yarm. Tom's own wherry, the *John Broadbent*, was 55ft long by 19ft 6in beam and drew about a foot unloaded. It was rigged with a loose footed main sail with a standing gaff and a foresail. The former was sheeted to a horse running across the deck in front of the helmsman. They had a long tiller to provide plenty of leverage on the rudder, 'otherwise [you] couldn't steer at speed.' There is a photograph in the Bowes Museum of three similar barges. They had a windlass forward which could handle warps as well as anchor chains.

4

HUMBER KEELS AND SLOOPS

Square-sailed Humber keels have been often been written about as being one homogenous type. However, the late Fred Schofield, a keel skipper and owner for many years, recorded ten varying types which were designed to different sizes and different rigs, according to where they operated. The West Country keels were 57ft 6in long and 14ft 2in beam and capable of making the transit across the Pennines, and were invariably towed by horses. Sheffield-sized keels measured 61ft 6in with 15ft 6in beam, and carried a single square sail and no leeboards. Manvers, Wath and Dearne keels ran to 57ft 6in and a 14ft 8in beam, and were towed, usually by a steam tug. The Barnsley type with a square main and topsail measured 70ft 4in by 14ft 4in, and the Driffield ones had a length of 61ft 4in and a beam of 14ft with two sails. Weighton keels were 5ft longer with the same beam and sails as the Driffield keels. Lincoln keels were 74ft 4in by 14ft 4in, again with two sails. Those of the Trent (known as 'catches' or ketches) were of the same dimensions as the Lincoln type, but built with a much sharper bow than all other keels, and with just the one sail and no leeboards. Horncastle keels were the shortest at 54ft 4in by 14ft 4in, with a single sail and leeboards. Finally, the Louth keels were 72ft long by 15ft beam, and carried a lug mizzen in addition to the two sails of the main mast (*Schofield, 1988: 2–4*). And then there were the gaff-rigged sloops and billyboys!

This litany demonstrates that within any one type of sailing barge, there often resides a host of variations. It also shows that the Humber gave access to a complex system of waterways, and many of these had different sized locks; these crucial dimensions were reflected in the build of the keels that traversed its water. The Ancholme Navigation and the River Hull and its branch navigations, such as the Driffield Canal, were the most easterly. Then, inland from Hull, there was the Trent to the south and all its connections with the narrow canals stretching across to the sea and the Midlands, as well as the rural waterways leading south to Lincoln, Horncastle and Sleaford. To the south-west, there was the River Don and the Sheffield Canal, linking that great steel town to outside trade. Due east, the Aire and Calder led to Leeds and the West Riding's industrial heartland. To the north-west, the Ouse carried keels to the old medieval port of York and up its tributaries – the Wharfe, the Ure and the Derwent. These

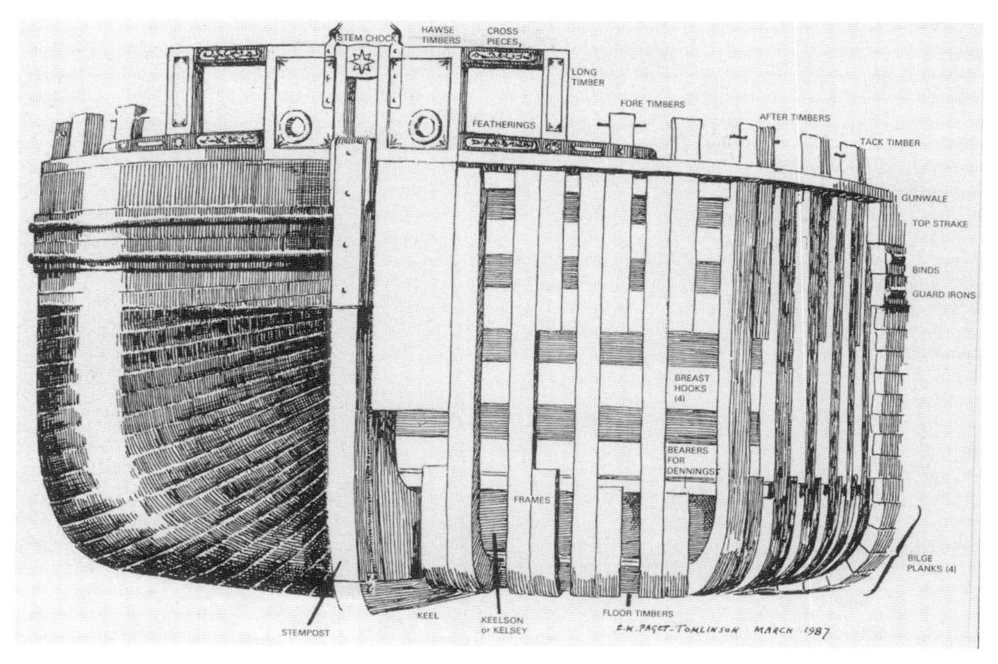

Keels were built with bluff bows and with the bow timbers at right angles to the side frames – an unusual method of framing. Overall, a wooden keel was stoutly built to withstand the strains of sitting on the mud and the knocks received in crowded docks. (E.W. Paget-Tomlinson)

The remains of an eighteenth-century keel found at St Aidan's open cast coal mine in 1997. (Mike Clarke)

There were hundreds of keels operating at the end of the nineteenth century, and Hull was one of their major centres because of the huge tonnage of imports that landed there which required transport inland. Note the clinker-built keel in the foreground.

waterways were progressively excavated, or made navigable by building locks, from the late seventeenth to the early nineteenth century. In addition, as overseas trade expanded and industrial production grew, Hull became an ever bigger entrepôt for imported raw materials. New docks such as those at Goole (1826), Grimsby (The Royal Dock , 1852) and Immingham (1912) expanded the accommodation for deep-sea shipping, and while some of the cargo went by rail, some of it went 'over the side' into keels for delivery inland.

This great network of waterways facilitated the carriage of a huge variety of cargoes. Schofield listed seventy-five different types of cargo that he had seen carried during his own lifetime in the twentieth century (*Schofield, 1988: 223–236*). Some were imports with exotic names including mimosa, myrobolams, quebracha and valerian. These were all natural products used in tanning leather. Then there were imports for specific industries such as gum arabic and various types of cocoa for the Rowntree's sweet factory at York, or metal ores such as chrome and tin, and chemicals such as sulphur. However, the staple cargoes were coal, corn, cattle food and timber. Coal was consumed in huge quantities by factories, the railways, and the growing number of steamers, including the booming fishing fleets of steam trawlers based at Hull and Grimsby from the late nineteenth century. It was also exported both coastwise and via deep sea. Wheat and barley were grown locally and imported from East Anglia. From about 1870 onwards, an increasing tonnage of wheat was shipped from North America, Australia and the Argentine to feed the growing urban population. Maize was another imported food crop, which fed both men and cattle. Huge quantities of linseed were brought in from the Baltic, and Hull was a centre for linseed oil extraction while the pressed

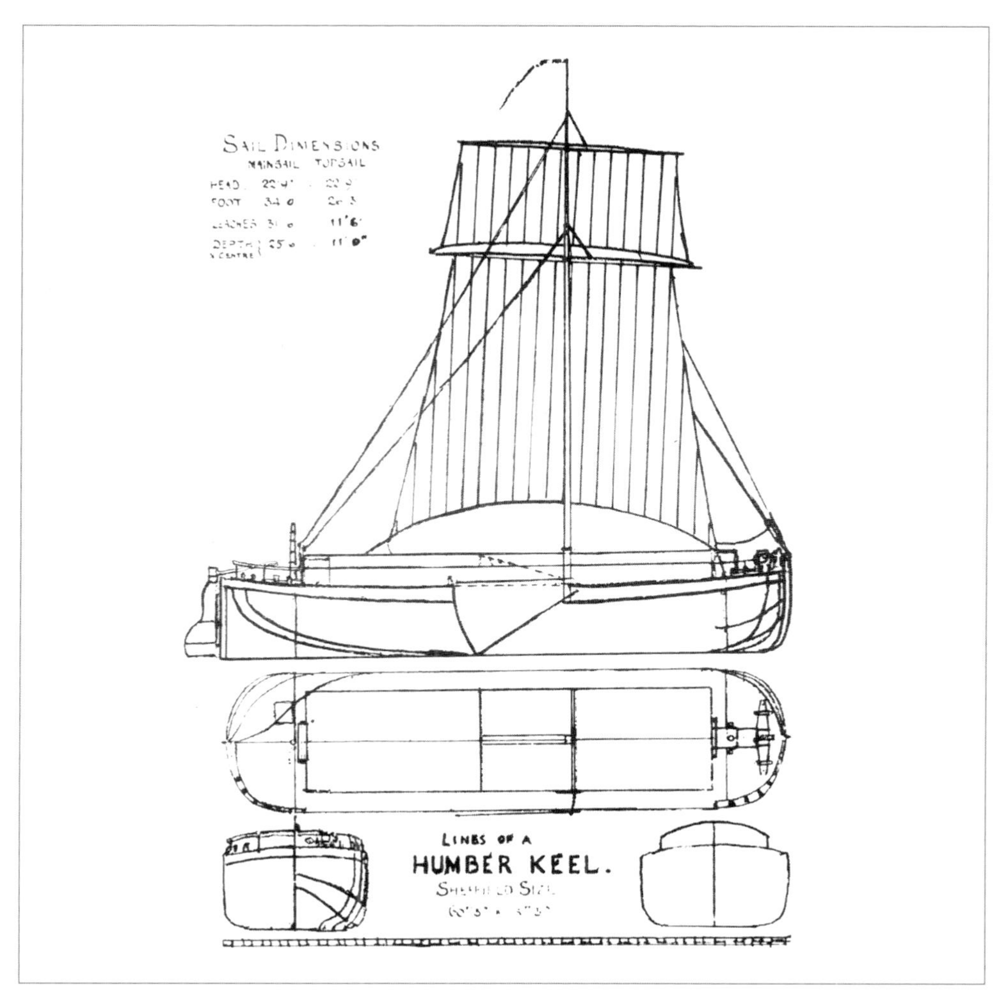

The lines and layout of a Humber keel as published in 1901.

residue made good cattle food. Timber from the Baltic and from Canada was imported mainly for use in the building trade, and locally made bricks from brickworks around the Humber, and sand from the Humber itself, all had to be carried in keels.

The Humber keel has always been seen as a descendant of medieval coasters. Certainly the clinker and carvel combination of building the hull could point to a descent from the medieval cogs, which dominated the North Sea trade from the thirteenth to the sixteenth centuries. Cogs had a similar form of construction with a flat bottom in carvel and clinker-built sides. However, their overall shape was different from the shallow bluff hull of the keel. The square sail rig and the pear-shaped deadeyes which tensioned the shrouds also harked back to the standing rigging found on late sixteenth-century vessels. Certainly clinker building for sailing barges, fishing boats and coasters was a local tradition along the East Coast in the eighteenth and nineteenth centuries. This covered large fishing luggers built from Yorkshire down to Great Yarmouth, keels and billyboys. The latter were a deeper but

Variations on the keel included the smaller Trent catch and the large Louth-size barge which carried a lug mizzen. (E.W. Paget-Tomlinson)

equally bluff-coasting version of the keel. Later keels and sloops tended to be carvel-built or of iron, and later steel, by the late nineteenth century. Wooden hulls were still being built up until the 1920s at the same time as the metal-hulled versions. West Country keels, which were an inland non-sailing keel, were still being built of wood up until the early 1950s.

However, there could be other variations in the construction of sailing barges. This is shown by the discovery, at St Aidan's open cast coal mine in 1997, of the remains of several keels found lying in the bottom of a redundant section of the River Aire. Archaeological excavations of these vessels and other structures revealed a total of eight vessels and an associated lock and dry dock. They appeared to have been tied up close to the dry dock, which presumably was a part of a shipyard. They had been largely dismantled, leaving the bottom of the hulls up to the turn of the bilge. The lower parts of their hulls were clinker-built and the upper planking was carvel, which is the complete reversal of what might have been expected. They measured around 55ft long with a beam of 12ft. This would have permitted them to have used the nearby Metheley Old Lock, work on which had been started in 1694. The discovery of a George II penny from 1755 between the inner and outer planking of one of the keels suggests that it must have been built before that date, as there is certainly no suggestion that it could have been washed into the hull. Further keel wrecks have also been investigated and recorded off Victoria Dock, Hull, and at Aldborough Flats, North Lincolnshire (*Buglass, 1997, 2000, 2001 & 2006*).

The hull form was double-ended with a flat bottom, round bilges and straight upright sides. There was a gentle sheer and the bows were almost square, while the stern was more rounded and was hollow below the waterline. The hull was very solidly built: the backbone was the keel

The *Comrade* is a Sheffield-size keel built in 1923 and preserved in sailing condition by the Humber Keel and Sloop Preservation Society. Her bluff bow and large hatch are clearly shown along with halliard rollers at the stern.

which was generally 12–14in across by 6in and the Kelsey (keelson), which was fastened on top of the frames, was a huge pitch pine baulk 12–14in square. This compensated for the inherent weakness caused by the large hatch which ran for most of the length of the keel. The frames were spaced at 9in centres and were in two pieces. The floors were 4in square and overlapped the futtocks at the bilge. The bow was so square that its frames were fastened at right angles to the rest of them. The hull planking was generally 2in-thick oak with extra thick planks at the turn of the bilge. The deck was supported on heavy deck beams which were fastened and supported by grown oak or iron brackets (knees). There was also a heavy covering board around the whole length of the hull that protected the tops of the frames from rot. Heavy wooden bollards for mooring were set into this at the bow and the stern (*Schofield, 1988*: 5–7).

The deck was dominated by the cargo hatch. Its coamings were about 2ft deep in the middle and the hatch opening was covered by about twenty-nine curved hatch covers – which in turn were protected by canvas tarpaulins. Right in the bow there was a heavy anchor windlass worked by pump levers and capable of handling two anchors. The chains of these were led through the hawse timbers. The stem chock between the two hawse timbers and the featherings and crosspieces, which connected the hawse timbers to the long timber, often had carvings on them. The stern rail and the tiller might also have been decorated with carvings. These bow timbers and the upper plank were also often painted into distinctive colours that were special to particular owners. Fred Schofield's, for example, had varnished or buff top strakes, with the rubbing bands picked out in black, and with blue on the hawseholes and other timbers with the carved sections picked out in black and gold.

The *Comrade* under full sail; with the port tack right forward and the starboard sheet aft, the sail can be finely trimmed to get as close to the wind as possible.

Raising the sails involved setting the top sail the first. The main sail which was stowed on deck had to be partly raised before the yard was swung round the shrouds for the final hoist.

The late Fred Schofield is working the *Comrade*'s top sail halliard roller in 1979.

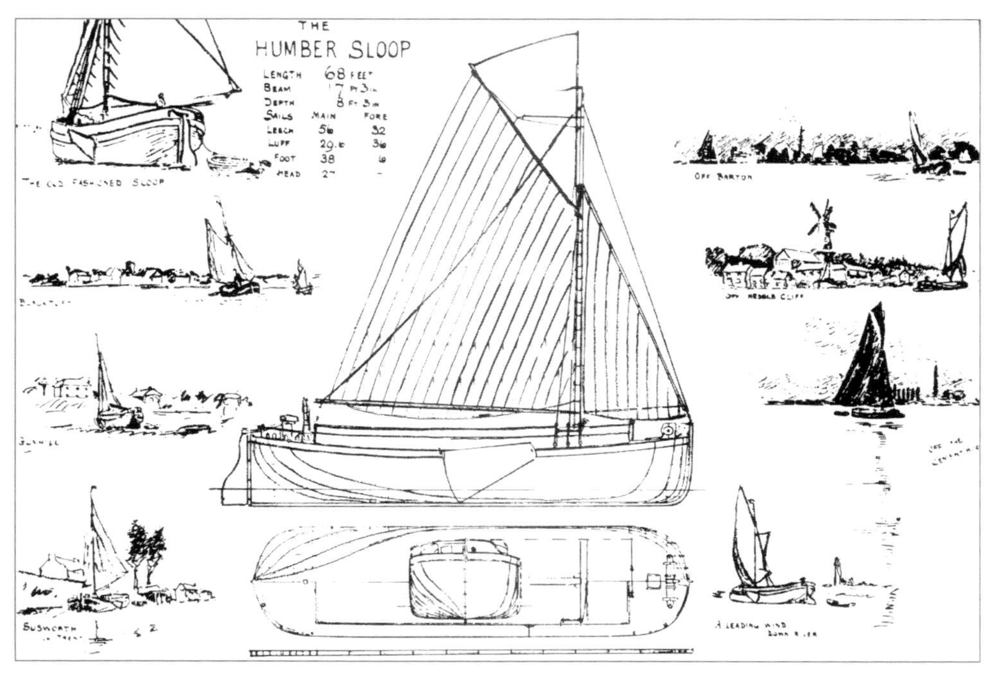

This plan of a 68ft sloop of 1903 shows the sloop's hull form is similar to the keel. The heavier mast is further forward and the main sail is sheeted close to the tiller. Earlier sloops had booms which projected over the stern which must have made it difficult to handle the main sail.

The foredeck also had a companion way which led to fo'c'sle cabin. This contained a cupboard bunk for a third crew member, if one was carried, along with the ship's stores of paint, rope, canvas, blocks etc., and a cast iron cooking range with an oven. The stern had a low rail and timber heads for mooring ropes. Earlier flats carried their water supply on two 30-gallon barrels chocked on either side. The main cabin was reached by means of a steep ladder from the companion way on deck. It was often panelled, grained and varnished, and, above a bench running part-way round the cabin, were two cupboard bunks and lockers for food, clothing and utensils. There was an open coal stove against the hold bulkhead and the cabin was lit by thick glass panels known as bull's-eyes let into the deck, and by a brass oil lamp. All very cosy, except for the fact that a keel man's life was one of long hours in all weathers. Wives were often carried and expected to assist with the sailing, as well as carrying out more domestic tasks.

The keel's mast was positioned in the lutchet – a stout post that went down to the keelson. It was supported by three shrouds and a back stay up to the topmast on either side. The forestay gave added support fore and aft, and a pair of blocks could be used to slack it off to allow the mast to be lowered to the hatch. All this rigging was made from wire rope on the latter-day keels. On inland trips where the sails would be of little use, the mast and sails were removed entirely and left on the canal bank. There was a main sail on all keels which was about 25ft deep at its centre and was curved along the length of its foot. Many keels also carried a topsail while a very few also carried a third – a topgallant-sail. Trent catches or ketches also carried a small lugsail mizzen. The sails were hoisted and controlled by hand winches, or 'rollers' as they were termed. This enabled a crew of two to operate so large a

The freshly painted sloop *Yokefleet*, built at Beverley in 1906 under sail. Note the unusual batten on the foot of the foresail. (H. Hodgson/Humber Keel and Sloop Preservation Society)

barge. The halliards which hoisted the sails and the slab line which used to take the drive out of the main sail were all led aft, so that the skipper on the tiller could control them. These had their own rollers with pawls to stop the rope slipping back out of control. There were also rollers for the sheets and the tacks. These pieces of rigging were made from a combination of wire rope and chain because they took a great deal of strain from the pressure of the wind as they held down the corners (clews) of the main sail. The topsail, which was about 11ft in depth, also had sheets running through blocks at the end of the main yard. The angle of the main yard was controlled by ropes attached at each end, which were known as braces.

When the keel was close-hauled or on a reach, one sheet would be led aft and the opposite tack led forward. This meant that the main sail and the top sail which followed its angle could be used almost like a lugsail. There was also a bowline which helped to hold up the windward side of the sail. This was particularly important when tacking and it called for fine judgement

Some coastal sloops and billy boys such as the *Ann*, of Goole, carried a bowsprit and square sails. The topmast stay sail is an unusual four-sided shape. In the background, there is another billy boy with three square sails set.

on the skipper's part as to when to order the mate to let the bowline go. It was so vital. In fact, all the keel's sailing operations, from raising the sails to lowering partially in bad weather to slowing down when entering a lock, called for a good deal of team work. This is brought out in Fred Schofield's book, which is based on his years of experience as a keel master and owner. The leeboards were also the other important piece of equipment. They replaced a deep keel or a centreboard. They prevented the keel from going to leeward. According to which tack the keel was on, a leeboard would be lowered, while the one on the other side of the hull was kept raised. They had their own rollers for raising and lowering. This was also important when sailing in shallow water because the leeboard that was down could be adjusted to the depth of water.

The sloop was a fore and aft rigged sister of the keel. It had the same hull form and there were instances of keels being converted into sloops and vice versa. They were not intended for inland navigation where the heavier sloop rig, especially the long boom of the main sail, would have been an inconvenience. A typical sloop in the early twentieth century was 68ft long with a beam of around 17ft and a depth 8–9ft. This made them too big for many of the inland waterways. But with a cargo capacity of around 170 tons they were capable of delivering cargoes coastwise. It is not clear when the sloop emerged as a separate type of sailing barge. Sloops and keels were drawn by the Buck brothers in their view of Hull in 1745. These vessels had raised sterns like the barges depicted on the Thames and do not seem to so bluff as their successors. As we have already seen, the Bucks aimed to be accurate and so these vessels are correct for the Humber in 1745. Sloops of the late eighteenth century

The sloop-rigged billyboy *Angerona* had the bluff clinker-built hull of an early nineteenth-century Humber vessel. Note she has much more sheer than a keel and solid bulwarks to make more suitable for coasting work. With their shallow draft billyboys could work inland to places like Leeds and Wakefield where they often delivered grain cargoes from East Anglia. (P. Catling/D. MacGregor Collection)

were heavily canvassed with a long main sail boom projecting over the stern, plus a foresail, a jib on a bowsprit, and a topsail and a square sail for running. Later sloops were simply rigged with fore and main sails. The sloops' build and layout were identical to the keel. Many had a continuous bulwark around the hull because they put to sea. The mast was stepped in the same way as a keel: well forward and could be lowered when required. There were rollers for handling the halliards and the sheets and a bowline on the foresail which was handy when tacking. Unlike the keels the sails were tanned.

According to John Leather, sloops could beat to windward when unloaded and in smooth water, but only slowly and in light weather, and could not be pinched (sailed too close to the wind) in any condition. Most were sailed best when trimmed slightly down by the bow, and when sailing in strong winds they had to be well reefed. If they missed stays and failed to tack, they had to gybe round, which is a fearsome process with such a large main sail (*Leather, 1984: 120–1*).

Sloops traded as far as Newcastle and London, but their main destinations tended to be nearer to home. The ports of Boston, King's Lynn, Wells and Blakeney were regular destinations. These served agricultural districts which needed coal and imported timber, fertilisers and cattle feed, and could supply back cargoes of wheat, barley and malt. The sloops needed at least three crew for such trips, but even so, the crew might consist of an experienced skipper and two youths learning the trade.

Billyboys were similar in their purpose and could be both larger and smaller than the sloops. They were originally clinker built and had deeper hulls which were quite bluff above the

Sons tended to followed fathers into keels. It was a hard life, but one that paid better than a shore job, and some keel men went on to become owners. It could be fatally hazardous as demonstrated by the grave stone of Arthur James Ward in Elloughton churchyard. He was drowned from the keel *Ebenezer* at Grimsby aged twenty-three years in 1897. He was mate to his father, James Ward of Brough. The memorial mason has made a fine job of depicting a keel and the cog boat. (David Cubitt)

water and quite fine below. The schooners, ketches and sloops that were built in Norfolk and Suffolk were similar in hull shape, though carvel built. They were also designed to sit on the mud at low tide and to withstand landing on open beaches where there were no harbours. But whether we should include them as a sailing barges is open to question. Although they performed the same function as the Humber sloops, they were confined to coastal waters. At the same time, the well-known Thames barges carried out both inland and coastal voyages.

Sloops and keels (and billyboys) were built in many places around the Humber. Major centres included Thorne, Hessle, Barton-on-Humber, Selby and Knottingley. For example, 214 sloops were launched at Knottingley between 1800 and 1870 (*Gosney and Bowyer, 2000*). Both sloops and keels raced in annual regattas in the nineteenth century. The race for the sloops continued until 1929, and sloops were still being built in the 1920s. There were seventy sloops sailing in 1933. The last wooden sloop, the *Peggy*, was launched from Clapson's yard at Barton on Humber in 1935 (*Laether, 1984: 132*). Many sloops and keels survived to be converted into motor barges. The steel-built keel *Comrade*, which had been built in 1923, has been restored to sailing condition, as has the sloop *Amy Howson* of 1914. Both are maintained and regularly sailed by the Humber Keel and Sloop Preservation Society. No original billyboy has survived. The Sobriety Trust has made a passable replica, the *Audrey*, from an old Humber lightship.

5

NORFOLK WHERRIES AND FENLAND LIGHTERS

Three rivers converge on Breydon water just inland from the Norfolk port of Great Yarmouth. The Bure and its tributaries go north and east and connect the market towns of Aylsham and North Walsham and the surrounding arable districts to the sea. The Yare flows from the west to connect Norwich, the capital of Norfolk, to the sea. To the south and the west, the Waveney runs past the towns of Beccles and Bungay. The Yare, the Bure and its attendant streams, the Thurne and the Ant, were connected with large shallow lakes known as Broads, and some of them provided access to quays at important villages such as Ranworth off the Bure or Surlingham off the Yare. The Broads have been proven to be flooded medieval peat workings. The Yare did not need locks, and the Waveney was made navigable beyond Beccles to Bungay with three locks in 1670. The upper reaches of the Bure above Coltishall were made navigable to Aylsham by five locks in 1779. The Ant was navigable to Dilham and then trade was opened to North Walsham via an artificial waterway – the North Walsham and Dilham Canal – which was finally completed in 1826. The 1833 opening of a canal between the Yare and the Waveney was part of a bigger scheme to enable seagoing vessels to go directly to Norwich via a new harbour at Lowestoft. This allowed them to bypass Great Yarmouth with its high tolls and transhipment costs. 12 miles further down the Suffolk coast, the River Blyth Navigation from Southwold to the market town of Halesworth opened in 1759. Cargoes on all these waterways were carried in keels and wherries.

In the west of the county, there was another extensive system of waterways, based around the rivers Ouse and Nene. They, and an extensive network of navigable artificial channels, drained a huge area of rich agricultural land progressively reclaimed from the marshes of the Fen District from the Romans onwards. The ports of King's Lynn and Wisbech served this hinterland, and lighters connected them to places as far distant as Bedford and Bury St Edmunds. The Fenland lighters, barges and turf boats were a completely different design to the Norfolk keels and wherries. The River Stour, on the boundary between Suffolk and Essex, was made navigable 25 miles from Brantham inland to the Suffolk town of Sudbury in about 1709. This navigation employed a type of barge that was similar in construction and

Two keels near Bishop's Bridge, Norwich, as depicted by the Buck Brothers in 1741.

shape to the Fenland lighter. Finally, there was another kind of sailing lighter which only operated within the confines of Blakeney harbour on the north Norfolk coast. Never numbering very many, they were mainly employed to lighter cargoes from seagoing ships anchored in the deep water of Blakeney Pit up to the quays at Blakeney, and at the much-silted port of Cley.

All these different waterways flourished as agricultural production expanded in the eighteenth century. The eastern counties were the 'bread basket' of the capital, which contained about 10 per cent of the country's total population. They also provided the malting barley from which its beer was brewed. The local barges delivered agricultural produce to seagoing coasters and collected coal, timber, cattle feed, fertiliser and a multitude of London shop goods for inland customers. Their traffic declined rapidly after the 1850s. Some was taken by railways which had penetrated much of the rural heartland by the end of the 1860s. Then, from about 1870, East Anglian farmers faced increasing competition from grain grown in North America, Argentina or Australia. Even though this was transported thousands of miles, it was still much cheaper than the home-produced crops. This great 'Agricultural Depression' had a knock-on effect on all the waterways of East Anglia.

There is every likelihood that the Norfolk keels of the eighteenth and nineteenth centuries were direct descendants of the sailing barges used on the rivers of Norfolk and Suffolk in the Middle Ages. However, the word 'keel' does not appear in local medieval records. For example, in 1343, the records of the Norwich Corporation mentioned the sinking of a boat bound for Norwich with the loss of thirty-eight lives (*Malster, 2003: 111*). On the other hand, the word 'keel' originates either from the Anglo-Saxon 'ceol' or the Norse 'kjoll' which both simply meant a boat, and so the use of the term 'keel' in later times could imply an earlier origin. They were certainly in existence by the sixteenth century, while in the early eighteenth century James Corbridge's map of Norwich, published in 1727, noted that keels of 40 and 50 tons could navigate up to Norwich. The Buck brothers' view of Norwich of 1741 showed several

Two early-nineteenth century wherries at Acle bridge. A lowering mast was essential because fixed bridges obstructed the navigation of all the rivers. The gaffs on these wherries were shorter than the later ones.

The keels were in rapid decline by the mid-nineteenth century, and with their open holds seemed to have been confined to hauling tree trunks, as this keel was pictured doing at Thorpe on the Yare just below Norwich.

A loaded wherry ice-bound, a hard time for wherrymen. The rig and deck layout are clearly seen. The sheer is also noticeable and a robin could certainly drink from the deck. (Bob Malster)

keels on the River Wensum. This flowed from its junction with the Yare at Trowse right through the heart of the city and was navigable as far as the New Mills. The Bucks showed one keel under a single square sail with a canvas tilt supported on semi-circular hoops. This suggests that it might have been a passenger carrier just like the unfortunate vessel of 1343. Another keel was shown with its mast lowered having shot through the main arch of Bishop's Bridge. This was one of several low bridges on the Norfolk waterways that would have been barriers to navigation, if it were not for the fact that the keels and the wherries all had lowering masts.

By the end of the eighteenth century the square-rigged keels were being replaced by wherries with gaff sails. The Norfolk wherries probably started as passenger vessels plying between Great Yarmouth and Norwich in the late seventeenth century. This was a time when the gaff rig was being widely adopted for inland and coastal sailing craft. The earliest mention of a wherry was in 1712, when a wherry carrying passengers to Norwich capsized and twenty people were drowned (*Malster, 1971: 58*). Its handier rig and smaller crew (two as against four on a keel) made it an effective competitor with the existing keels. In 1795, a register of inland vessels drawn up by the town clerk of Great Yarmouth covered 149 craft, with another seven added up to 1798 when the record finished. There were thirty-four keels which varied in size from 20 to 97 tons, and 134 wherries (*Malster, 2003: 115*). In 1831, the anonymous *Norfolk Tour* remarked that keels 'were chiefly restricted to the freightage of timber and are far less numerous than formerly'. Several of the early nineteenth century views of the River Yare show keels carrying tree trunks in their open holds and the last one under sail (the *Dee Dar* – an odd name that has never been explained) was used to transport logs up to Norwich. Others were turned into dumb barges to carry the spoil from dredgers.

A wherry taking cargo off one of the coasters of the General Steam Navigation Co. at Great Yarmouth. Wherries delivered many cargoes to inland destinations and especially to Norwich.

They were extinct by 1900. The remains of several keels survived, sunk into the side of the River Yare to reinforce its banks.

Keels had similar proportions to the later wherries. For example, the *Dee Dar* measured 55ft in length by 13ft 8in beam with a draft of 4ft. Another un-named keel abandoned in a partially sunk condition at Postwick Grove (on the Yare just below Norwich) measured 54.5ft by 14.5ft with a depth of 4.2ft. Her dimensions and detailed plan were used to build a model for the Science Museum, and also presumably the one for the Bridewell Museum, Norwich. The keel's hull was clinker built but unlike the wherry had a small transom stern; the hold was entirely open – very much a characteristic of barges of early origin – and the crew's cabin was located in the bow instead of the stern. The low mast carried a single square sail and was placed amidships, and could be lowered by slacking off the tackle at the stem end of the forestay. As well as its forestay, the mast was supported by a shroud on each side.

The two aforementioned models were the only three-dimensional evidence of the keel until 1985. In that year a buried keel at Whitlingham marshes just outside Norwich was excavated and recorded (*Douglas-Sherwood, 1993: 346–8*). It was then raised and brought to Norwich and placed under a plastic tent. Unfortunately, conservation was not started immediately and the keel remained under its plastic tent in a deteriorating condition. It then had to be moved to another site and at the time of writing it has deteriorated very badly. This is a pity, because if it had been properly cared for it would have been a unique exhibit for the new Broadlands Museum.

The wherry seems to have started as a passenger vessel running between Great Yarmouth and Norwich. The Thames had passenger wherries from an early date, and these were light

Delivery upriver – a wherry unloading at Stalham Staithe. Note how the boom has been swung clear and the curved hatch covers are stacked clear of the hold. The heavy tiller and the companionway to the cabin aft are also visible.

The wherry's tall tanned sail and mast can seen at Wroxham about 1900. This was a trading wherry that had been converted for pleasure cruising, with the hatch raised with a line of windows to make a spacious and well lit set of cabins.

Raising the black tanned sail with the winch. Wherries, like other barges, provided plenty of work for their minimal crews. When freight became scarce some skippers would manage a wherry on their own.

clinker-built vessels mainly intended for rowing rather than out-and-out sailing craft. They were London's taxis. Closer to the Yare, the River Orwell in Suffolk had passenger wherries which linked Ipswich and Harwich. These were large-decked, two-masted spritsail vessels. The Norfolk version, by the eighteenth century, had a boomless, single large gaff-rigged main sail. Early nineteenth-century pictures of wherries show these craft with a short gaff; but this evolved during the nineteenth century to the characteristically long gaff. This could be as much as 40ft long, and supported the high-peaked black sail. The latter got its colour from a tanning mixture of coal tar and fish oil to preserve its canvas from rot. This tall sail was designed to catch the slightest tremor of a breeze above the trees that grew on the river banks in many places. The sail was hooped to a stout mast which was usually fashioned from a baulk of pitch pine about 45–50ft long. It was placed well forward, clear of the hold, and was pivoted to allow it to be lowered for passing under fixed bridges. Its bottom was fitted

The wherry carried decorative name boards and a wind vane, often with a cut out figure and a long length of red bunting. (Norfolk Museums Service)

with a counterweight of about a ton of lead. When the forestay was slackened the mast could be lowered quickly and safely. The throat and peak halliards were linked together so that the sail could be hoisted in one action with the help of a winch mounted in front of the mast. The mast was reliant on its own strength and the support of the forestay to withstand the enormous leverage exerted by the large sail. However, it was not unknown for masts to break at the deck, especially under stress when competing at local regattas.

Wherries could also vary in size. There were little 'market' wherries and wherries that went all the way up the shallow River Ant. These could be as small as the 14-ton *Lark*, of Irstead, of 1795, and as massive as the 90-ton *Wonder* of 1878, which was used to lighter cargoes from ships anchored in Yarmouth Roads. The average size for a wherry was around 40 tons and measured about 57ft long by 14ft beam with a depth in the hold of 4ft. They were clinker built and double-ended. There are one or two photographs which show wherries with transom sterns, but they were unusual. It is possible that the transom-sterned wherries were in fact keels converted to wherry rig. There were later wherries built of iron rather than oak, and one wherry, the *Albion*, was carvel built at Bungay in 1898. Ironically, she was the last trading wherry available in reasonable condition and was purchased by the Norfolk Wherry Trust in 1948.

Wherries were built largely of oak, with grown frames and 2in-thick planks, with usually fourteen on each side of the hull. The hull was dish-shaped and this can be seen well in the photograph of the *Albion* under repair at Lowestoft (see image no.9, colour section). The keel was around 9in deep and some had an additional slipping keel which could be removed without taking the wherry out of the water, allowing for trading at the shallower upper reaches. The hull had a lot of sheer and the raised out deck plank (known as the plank sheer and not the covering board) was painted white as a safety measure. The iron rubbing strake around the

The last wherries were converted into motor or dumb barges. The *I'll Try* was still at work for Thains on the River Bure in 1962. She and others like her were soon replaced by steel motor barges.

outside of the hull was known as the binns. When a wherry was well-loaded down to the binns, the water lapped the covering board amidships 'so that a robin could drink off the deck'.

The curved stem was normally painted with a white quadrant. According to old wherrymen, this was to make the wherry visible at night to other craft underway. G. Colman Green, an early writer on the wherry, stated that these 'eyes' were a late manifestation of the ships' *oculi* 'derived from ancient usage as far back as the Egyptian civilisation of the XX Dynasty' (*Colman Green, 1953: 29*). But that seems somewhat fanciful for a down-to-earth county like Norfolk, and besides there was no continuity between Ancient Egyptian and nineteenth-century English craft. However, it was a device that was perpetuated on the steel dumb lighters built in the 1890s and early 1900s for towing between Great Yarmouth and Norwich. It was even found on the steel 'motor wherries' that were built in the 1960s to replace worn-out wooden wherries.

The single hold was open on the keels. The wherries offered better protection and greater capacity with built-up coamings or 'right ups'. The shifting 'right ups' were a removable top section. They were topped off with curved hatch covers, each built to overlap with the next one which provided (when in good condition) a completely watertight cover for the hold. The standing 'right ups' were painted in blue and the shifting ones white, with the hatch covers and the cabin roof (continuous with the covers) in red. Other items of equipment, including the halliard winch and the rigging blocks, were also painted red. The gaff was white and the mast was varnished. Its top section was usually painted blue and for recognition the owners' colours in horizontal bands were painted between the blue and the varnish. The 'herring hole', the halliard sheave pin bearing, was painted with a star or some other devices. The forward end of the coamings had painted panels with the wherry's name and that of the

The Bucks depicted a train of Fenland lighters in the foreground of their 'prospect' of Ely of 1743. The forelighter carried a large square sail as well as being towed by two horses. It was followed by another three lighters.

owner, often in fancy lettering. The final decorative flourish was the wind vane which had often had a decorative figure or letter cut out of metal with a long red pennant (the lag) flying from it. So, for example, the *Jenny Morgan* had a silouhette of a Welsh girl holding a bunch of daffodils. All this paintwork and decoration made the Norfolk wherry much more colourful than other sailing barges.

Some of the details of the wherry's rig have already been mentioned. The black sail could be extended by an extra strip of canvas (a bonnet) along its bottom. There is also a painting of wherries racing and carrying foresails, but this was unusual (*Clark, 1961: 48*). The sail could be trimmed from the steering cockpit aft. It could also be reefed or the peak of the sail lowered to take some of the 'drive' out of the sail during squalls. The wherry was reasonably handy in tacking, although sometimes the mate would help the bow round with a quant. This was a 22ft-long punt pole which was plunged in at the bow, pressed against the shoulder and walked aft to propel the wherry when the wind did not serve. Wherrymen had to consider the tide which penetrated well inland. At Great Yarmouth, it ran especially fast where the Bure joins the Yare and through the Haven Bridge, which wherries would run under with lowered masts. It was common practice to use a weight on a rope to 'dredge' using the power of the tide to move.

The wherry's crew of two lived while working in a compact cabin right aft. There was space for two bunks which served as seats and a coal stove. The married ones usually had a cottage ashore, though it was not unknown for wives to accompany their husbands on trips.

9 The pleasure wherry *Hathor* of 1903 being quanted with her mast lowered under Bishop's Bridge in the 1990s. (Andrew Worman)

10 The surviving wherry *Albion* on the slipway at Lowestoft in 2003 gives a good idea of the graceful shape of the wherry's hull. Note the white painted patches on the bow.

11 *Above:* The *Mirosa* of 1892, under sail near Orford, is one of two barges that do not have engines. She is using the tide as much as the wind to proceed to the sea.

12 *Left:* Furling the main sail on the *Pudge*, using the brails to draw the sail into the mast. The top sail has already be dropped. The tackle of the port vang is in the foreground and the main sheet has been released to allow the sail to be furled.

13 *Opposite above:* The *Alice Watts* of 1875 was a typical early boomie barge with a curved bow and counter stern and double square top sails along with fore and aft top sails. (Harwich Maritime Museum)

14 *Opposite below:* Later boomie barges were built with straight bows and transom sterns like the *Thalatta* of 1906. She was later converted to sprit rig with a mulie mizzen and is a youth training ship now.

15 The *Shamrock* being prepared for her winter laying up at Cotehele in October 2006. Wooden hulls, especially old ones, need constant maintenance. Note the main mast in its tabernacle and the large cast-iron, multi-purpose winch.

16 The *Shamrock* under sail off Plymouth on one of her sailing trials. (The National Trust)

This late eighteenth-century view of Bedford Bridge shows a lighter with a substantial rig with standing rigging. The open hold with the separating bulkheads can be clearly seen.

Along with sailors, bargees and fishermen, wherrymen were regarded as a heathen lot and church missions were set up in the nineteenth century to enlighten them. A Wherrymen's Mission was established at Great Yarmouth in 1857 with a reading room and a chapel close to the quay on the Bure. Wherries were owned by local firms such as coal and corn merchants with the occasional skipper/owner. Both steam towage with large steel barges and the railways took over an increasing volume of cargo in the late nineteenth century. By the end of the nineteenth century, the Norfolk Broads were becoming a tourist destination. Some wherries were converted for cruising, and several new pleasure wherries were built. The *Albion* was the last to carry cargoes under sail in the 1950s, but the Wherry Trust found it did not pay. A few survived as motor or dumb barges for carrying dredgings or sugar beet. There are seven wherries afloat today but only three were built as cargo carriers.

The Fenland lighters might have been narrow clinker built and double-ended, but they bore no resemblance to the Norfolk wherries. The largest were 47ft long with a beam of 10ft and could carry about 20 tons. Then there were smaller versions 27ft long, and there was also a smaller punt about 16–18ft long. One of these punts has been preserved at the National Maritime Museum, Cornwall. A few of the large lighters built at the end of the nineteenth century were carvel built and one of them was raised from the Roswell clay pits near Ely in 1972. The standard hull was formed from broad 15in oak planks tapering to 8in at the bow and stern. They were flat bottomed with a sharp bilge and a slight tumblehome. There was no decking, just two open holds and four deck beams (*Jenkins, 1993: 158*).

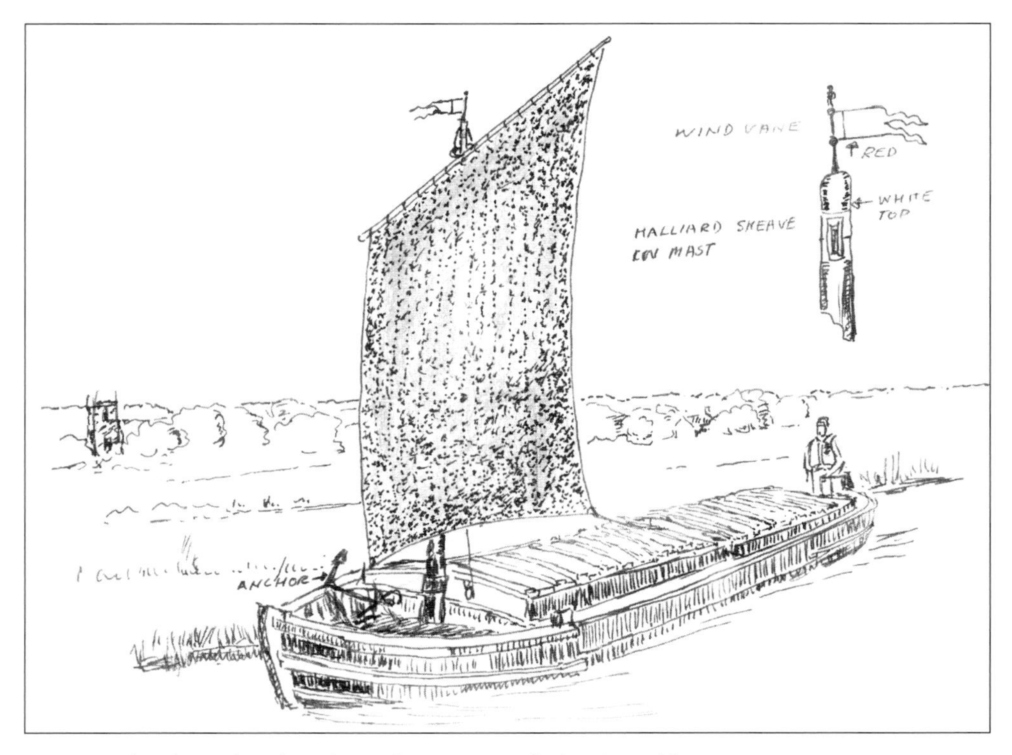

A Stour sailing barge, based partly on the paintings of John Constable.

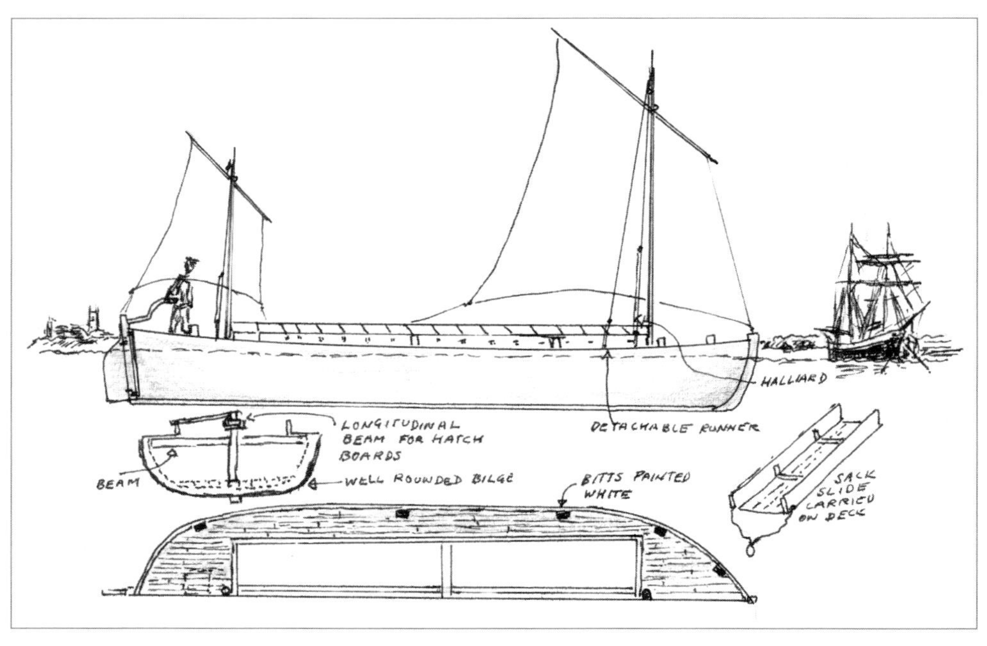

A Blakeney harbour sailing lighter, based on photographs and the registered dimensions of the *Glaven* of 1841.

The lighters were worked in groups of up eight lighters, although four or five seem to have been the norm. They were chained closely together and there was a large spar (the jambing pole) projecting from the second onto the fore lighter. This could be used to steer the 'train'. Normally lighters were towed by horses, and in later years by tugs. In the eighteenth and early nineteenth centuries the 'fore lighter' carried a mast with a square sail. This was used in conjunction with the horses and can be seen in the Bucks' view of Ely of 1743. The sailing lighters were never photographed and so it is difficult to say much about their rigging. A late eighteenth-century print of Bedford bridge has a lighter in the foreground with a tall mast with three shrouds on each side of the hull, and braces on the yard which is hoisted aloft without a sail. It is impossible to know how accurate this picture is. Certainly the hull details are correct. The smaller lighters plying singly sometimes carried a basic spritsail. The lighters on the River Stour were of similar design and dimensions to the Fenland type, and were towed in twos by horses and were fitted with hatch covers. In the early nineteenth century they were also sailed singly, when the wind was favourable. Thanks to John Constable we know they were rigged with a single lugsail. This was especially useful on the tidal waters below Brantham, when they went to load at Mistley.

Blakeney harbour on the north Norfolk coast served two small ports – Blakeney and Cley. Both suffered from silting as tidal marshlands were progressively reclaimed and the volume of water to clear away silt was reduced. Nevertheless, they both had a thriving traffic in exporting barley and wheat and importing coal, up to the middle of the nineteenth century. Deeply loaded ships were lightened by sailing lighters. By the time they were photographed in the late nineteenth century, there were: the *Clam*, *Only Son*, *Tigris*, *Lion* and *Yankee*. The former two had sails and the latter ones were towed by a tug. The *Clam* had been built as a Thames lighter with a lugsail. She survived as a houseboat into the 1970s. The others were various shapes and sizes. In 1909, the billyboy *Bluejacket* (1860) was converted into a lighter (*Hooton, 1997: 258*). The two lighters photographed at Cley in the 1880s may have been locally built versions. One was found in the Ship Registers for Cley. The *Glaven* was built in 1841 by Thomas Claxton at Blakeney, and measured 19 tons, 43.4ft length, 13.1ft beam and 4ft depth of hold. She was rigged as a two-masted lugger and was owned by two millers living near Cley. This description fits in with the two lighters that were photographed. They were double-ended and carvel built with a rounded hull and a flat sheer. There was a large single hatch with low coamings and hatch boards which rested on a central beam, and bollards painted white along each side of the hull. There was a tall lugsail on the forward side of the hatch and a smaller one right aft. I have tried to incorporate all these features in a sketch plan of the *Glaven*. These sailing barges are the least-known type I have come across, and there are doubtless others that operated in a very limited range on other estuaries and in other ports, and have not been fully recorded.

6

THAMES BARGES

The early sailing barges on the River Thames and its tributaries have already been briefly discussed in Chapter Two. The survival of large structural fragments going back to the Roman occupation, and dating through to the Middle Ages, show that London's commercial dependence on its river and barges was long-standing. Three centuries ago the Buck brothers' engravings provided visual evidence of how the capital and its shipping had expanded. These panoramas showed punt-like barges with swim-headed bows, budget sterns and square sails, as well as more seaworthy ones. The latter were generally described as hoys. The Bucks' views of Reading and Oxford – towns on the Thames inland from London – showed more of the square-sailed barges. In addition to the upriver and coastal barges, large number of lighters were required to ferry cargo between ships moored in the Pool of London and waterfront quays and warehouses. Most of these latter barges managed without sails, relying on the power of the tide and long sweeps.

The barge which is recognised as a Thames barge today only really reached this final form in the late nineteenth century. This produced a versatile craft which was capable of trading coastwise and upriver with a good cargo capacity and the minimum of crew. These virtues and the continuing availability of cargoes helped the Thames barge outlast all the other types of sailing barge in commercial traffic. Before the surviving type of Thames barge emerged, there were also swimmies, stumpies, lug boats and boomies. The photographs of the Pool of London taken by George Washington Wilson in the 1870s show a wide range of barges employed on the Thames. So, for example, the lug boats were not only lug rigged but they could be built as both swim-headed and round-ended, clinker or carvel built, decked or undecked. Many had clear affinities to medieval vessels (*Ellmers, 1996*).

London's population by 1700 was over half a million, or 10 per cent of the total population of England, and by 1800 it was well on the way to a million. By 1901, Greater London had 6.5 million people, a fifth of the total for England and Wales (*Inwood, 1998: 270 &413*). Such a growing concentration of people in an urban centre required food, fuel, building materials and much else, in increasing quantities. Many of these commodities could be delivered in

The hoy was the predecessor of the Thames barge in the coastal trade in and around the Thames estuary.

bulk cheaply by water, and sailing barges were one of the main forms of transport that fuelled this booming city. Corn and other agricultural produce were carried from neighbouring counties, as were bricks, cement and timber. Barges also distributed manufactures, imports and horse droppings for fertiliser to outlying areas. In 1796, a House of Commons report on the London Docks recorded that there were 3,397 assorted barges, lighters, punts and lug boats cluttering the Thames (*Ellmers, 1996*).

The development of docks downstream from the Pool in the nineteenth century provided further opportunities for sailing barges. Imported grain, including wheat and maize, was distributed by barges from the docks to mills mainly along the East Coast, from the Wash down to east Kent. Some millers – such as the Cranfield Brothers and R.&W. Paul at Ipswich, Green Brothers of Malden or E. Marriage & Son of Colchester – owned and managed their own barges, and the same applied to the Kentish brick and cement makers such as Eastwoods (brick makers) and Associated Portland Cement Manufacturers (Blue Circle Cement). Many of their cargoes were destined for very small ports well inland such as Norwich. Decline in sailing barge traffic probably began at the end of the nineteenth century. Rail transport was their main competitor, but new barges were still being built up to the 1920s (though in decreasing numbers). There were an estimated 2,000 in 1910 and by 1939 the total had declined to about 750. Road transport and the Depression of the early 1930s had thinned out the numbers, and after the losses of the Second World War there were just 125 left under sail. There were also quite a number which had lost most of the sails and

An early nineteenth-century swim-headed boomie barge loaded with tree trunks.

were propelled by diesel or petrol engines (*Benham, 1951: 20*). By 1995, the Society for Sailing Barge Research listed forty-five barges which still had their sails. None of them carried commercial cargoes. Some were privately owned, some earned a living by taking passengers on sailing trips, and some were permanently tied up in docks as bars or restaurants.

The need to carry cargoes on the Thames estuary and the neighbouring coasts called for barges that were more seaworthy than the square-sailed lighter with an open hold. Two solutions seem to have been developed in the late sixteenth or early seventeenth century. The first was to equip flat-bottomed swim-headed barges with leeboards and fore and aft sails. The other was the hoy, which was perhaps more of coaster than a barge. The lighter had a completely flat bottom with the sides at a sharp angle known as a 'chine'. The Bucks showed plenty of hoys downriver from London at places such as Gravesend, Deptford or Rochester. On the basis of a plan of a hoy dating from somewhere between 1750 and 1775, now located in the Science Museum, the hoy's hull had a much more rounded bottom and a fine bow and stern below the waterline. The latter two characteristics combined with a flat bottom to define the hull form of the typical later nineteenth-century Thames barges. A plan of a sailing barge built at King's Lynn for the Admiralty in the same period had flatter floors but the same general proportions. The former measured 50ft 6in by 17ft 3in with a depth of 7ft 5in, and the latter 70ft by 19ft 6in with a depth of 9ft 5in. Hoys, with their finer deeper hulls, did not carry leeboards. They were kept busy sailing between ports such as Ipswich and Colchester to the north, and Rochester and Faversham to the south. For example, they

Some swim-headed spritsail barges were used for coastal passages. E.W. Cooke pictured this barge in 1828 with a lifting bowsprit and a square sail.

Swimmie barges with stump masts and tillers were still to be found on the Medway and the Thames, just like one tied up in front of a topsail barge at Sheerness Dockyard in 1910. (Marine & Cannon Books)

The structure of a Thames barge is illustrated by the derelict remains of an unknown barge at Bembridge, Isle of Man. The keelson, frames, chine and the internal planking (ceiling) are visible along with some of the deck beams.

carried wheat, barley, beans and oats from the Kentish ports of Sandwich and Faversham. Between 1 October 1757 and 25 June 1758 a total of 786 shipments were made to London from these two ports (*Baker, 1970: 126–150*). These hoys also took passengers and carried shop goods such as textiles and spices back from London. The hoy's rig consisted of a main sail set on a standing gaff, without a boom and a foresail and a jib. This meant that the sail could be easily furled using brails – lines which were used to pull the sail up to the mast and the gaff. This labour-saving device was also used on the spritsail – more on that shortly.

While there was variety of build and rig, the main kind of barge by the end of the nineteenth century was the round-bowed, transom-sterned spritsail barge that is so familiar to us in the twenty-first century. It is not clear how they developed from the rather clumsy 'swimmie' lighter into a more sea-kindly shape. In open waters the flat bow of the 'swimmie' banged into the seas which made them difficult to handle, especially as they were normally steered with a tiller. Earlier writers have suggested that the establishment of barge races in 1863 was the major stimulus to improving the hull form. More recent research in the Shipping Registers of Ports in Essex and north Kent has shown that there was already a substantial fleet of round-bowed spritsail barges in existence by the last decades of the eighteenth century (*Perks, 2004: 48–9*). These must have been substantial seagoing craft.

The changes in the economics of transport after 1850 may also have played a part in the development of the Thames barge. As railways took traffic away from small coastal ports, and as English agriculture became increasingly depressed by the cheaper imports and poor

The sharp chine, the fine entrance and run aft can be clearly seen in the *George Smeed* of 1882. One of the oldest surviving barges, the *George Smeed* was built for the same owners that built several very large square-rigged barges.

harvests, the East Anglian and Kentish fleets of brigs, schooners and sloops with their crews of four or five and their deep draught became less and less viable as commercial carriers. The Thames sailing barges with their 'go-anywhere' draught and small crew seem to have gradually replaced these older types. At the same time there was still a good tonnage of freights needing transport to London. These ranged from straw and hay from Essex, to bricks and cement from Kent. Millers in the provincial ports required wheat or maize brought from abroad by large cargo steamers into the London Docks, and many barges had a steady trade carrying these cereals. Coal could still be carried economically by sea, and the smaller East Coast ports provided coal freights for barges which usually loaded Yorkshire coal at ports on the Humber such as Goole and Keadby. In fact, the range of barges continued to expand right up to 1914. Thames barges were seen in West Country ports loading china clay, in near Continental ports and even up the Rhine to load consignments of Apollinaris mineral water.

Thames barges increased in size from the late eighteenth to the early twentieth century. A plan of a swim-headed 'English chalk barge', published in Chapman's *Architectura Navalis* in 1768, was 55ft long, 17ft 6in beam and 5ft depth. The surviving barges give a pretty good cross-section of the typical dimensions of barges. The *Centaur*, for example, which is still sailed by the Thames Barge Sailing Club, was built in 1895 at Harwich and measures 85ft 6in by 19ft 6in with a depth of 6ft 3in. These dimensions were fairly typical for barges built in the late nineteenth century. The biggest barges ever built were the four built at Great Yarmouth for F.T. Everard in 1926. The only survivor, the *Will* (formerly the *Will Everard*)

The *Pudge* of 1922 at Whitstable shows off the classic layout and rig of a stay sail barge. Note the bow decoration, and the height of the mast with its sprit and the starboard leeboard.

The main sheet was hauled tight by a tackle and secured to a ring that runs across the horse. The low bulwark and the quarter rail above it can be seen behind the horse.

is built of steel and measures 97ft 6in by 23ft by 9ft 6in. These dimensions gave her a maximum cargo capacity of nearly 200 tons. The gaff-rigged 'boomie' barges also tended to be larger than their 'sprittie' sisters. The *Thalatta* was built at Harwich in 1906 as a 'boomie' and measures 88ft 10in by 20ft 6in with a depth of 7ft. She was later converted to sprit rig which saved one (and on occasions two) of her original complement of four men. There were a few even more giant vessels built on barge lines and rigged as schooners, barquentines or barques. The earliest recorded was the 275-ton barge/barque *Louisa Shelburne*, launched at Battersea in 1853 (*MacGregor, 1984: 112*). George Smeed, a Sittingbourne builder and barge owner, launched the biggest: the 494-ton barque *Esther Smeed* in 1868. He used this extraordinary 'barge' in the Baltic trade until it was wrecked in 1878 (*Sattin, 1990: 52–3*).

At the other end of the scale, there were very small barges for inland or estuary work. The *Lady of the Lea* was built in 1931 and was the last sailing barge ever built. She was owned by

Barges were built in many sizes. The *Cygnet* of 1881, moored at Snape, at 16 tons was among the smallest. Note the typical decoration on the stern.

the Ministry of Defence and was intended to carry explosives from the Waltham Abbey gunpowder works down the Lea Navigation. She measured 72ft long with a beam of only 13ft (so that she could fit through the locks on the Lea). The *Cygnet* (as her name suggests) was even smaller. She was built in 1881 for Walter Wrinch, a farmer at Erwarton on the Stour estuary, and had a registered tonnage of only 16 tons.

While the barges' hull form had developed what would become its final, settled form, there were notable variations within its main parameters. Coasting barges tended to be given more sheer and higher bulwarks than river barges, for obvious reasons. The mainstay for Essex barges was 'the stack' trade. Straw and hay were needed in huge quantities for the thousands of horses of London. These cargoes were carried on deck (sometimes almost half way up the mast) as well as in the hold, because of their high volume and low weight. As a result, 'stackies', as they were nicknamed, tended to be built with a greater beam, shapely ends and with little sheer. Some builders adopted a more scientific approach to hull design. Howard of Maldon, who was a qualified naval architect, is credited with being the first barge builder to design his products on paper rather than using a half-model and experience (*Benham, 1951: 137*). Most barges were built with a straight stem. A few of the ketch-rigged boomie barges were built with curved stems and counter sterns. However, a flat transom stern was typical for all kinds of barge. Its shape could vary according to its builder. The barges built by J. & H. Cann at Harwich (who had the reputation for building the best barges) had a shallow broad transom, while those built by some of the Rochester and Kent builders had much deeper narrow sterns. The counter stern on the *Haughty Belle* of 1896 was unique among the spritsail barges and her owners specified this, along with finer than usual lines, in order to outwit rival owners in the fiercely contested barge races.

The bow and stern of most barges were embellished with bow and quarter boards, along with the transom. The bow and quarter boards were carved with incised tendrils, often

Boomie barges traded to more distant ports. Some such as the *Ivy P*, which was photographed with three dumb flats in Canning Dock, Liverpool were sold off to owners distant far from the Thames.

The lug bridge sail was an essential piece of equipment for the barges that plied up the Thames.

The barges that survived the Second World War were gradually converted to auxiliaries or pure motor barges. The *Oxygen* of 1895 was cut down to a stumpie rig when she called at Norwich in 1959.

picked out in yellow against a green background. The latter were on each side of the stern. The barge's name was also incised on each side of the bow, sometimes on a ribbon. There was also an incised line picked out in yellow running along the bulwarks. At the stern, there was a topgallant rail on top of the bulwark which was invariably painted white. The transom carried the barge's name on the left and the port of registry and sometimes the owner's name on the right. These letters were normally carved into the transom timbers and might be accompanied by some more tendrils. J. & H. Cann's barges all had their names and registry ports on ribbons draped over a double-headed arrow. The wooden barges' hulls were invariably black. Some of the iron- and steel-hulled ones had different colours. The London & Rochester Shipping Co. painted their barges and coasters in a red oxide colour, while the Horlock barges from Mistley had grey hulls.

The strength of the hull depended on a flat keel which was usually about 14in wide by 4–5in deep. This was strengthened by a massive keelson. This could be baulk of pine up to 18in square. Later wooden barges had a steel girder instead of the wooden keelson. The floors (bottom frames) were sandwiched between these two components and were fastened to the heads (upright frames). The planks where the sides joined the bottom (the chine) were thicker timbers which provided added longitudinal support. Inside the frames there was an inner set of planking with heavier longitudinal timbers at the bottom and at deck level. The deck was laid on heavy crossbeams which could be as much as 15in by 4in. Those between the two hatches also carried the weight of the main mast, the sprit, main sail and

The biggest of all the spritsail barges, the *Will Everard* (later the *Will)* still survives. She was one of four built in 1925. This mulie barge made many long coastal voyages as well as trips to continental ports such as Calais and Rotterdam.

topsail. The deck beams were supported by grown oak or wrought iron brackets known as knees. There were two hatches and there was accommodation in the bow for the mate and the third hand, if one was carried. The skipper lived aft, often in wood-panelled splendour. Some of the coastal barges were equipped with a wheelhouse which incorporated a lavatory at its stern end.

Barges carried a series of winches to assist their minimal crew. Right in the bow there was a low-geared windlass for raising the anchor, with a smaller winch above it which could be used to help lower the main mast. At the foot of the mast there were two winches to assist with the top sail running rigging when necesssary, and a dedicated winch for hauling in the main brail to draw the main body of the main sail into the mast. Aft there were two more winches to handle the tackles that raised and lowered the lee boards. Spritsails were not unique to Thames barges, but in this country no other vessel carried such large spars. The sprit (usually pronounced 'spreet') was rigged diagonally from the foot of the mast to the upper corner of the main sail. This meant that the sail was kept permanently aloft and was furled by a set of five brails. The sprit is held to the mast by a heavy chain and supported by a wire rope – the stanliff. Its upper end is controlled by two more wires with tackles leading down aft which were known as vangs (pronounced 'wangs'). The sprit, with all its weight and that of the sail far aloft, had to be kept steady, especially in windy conditions. Wooden sprits had been known to break under strain and all the surviving barges have steel sprits. The sail is controlled by the sheet – a tackle

Barge yachts such as the *Boojum* of 1907 were built along barge lines in the early 1900s and were popular on the South and East Coasts of England.

hooked into its after lower corner and running across the barge on a bowed and horizontal wooden (or later iron) pole known as a horse.

The main mast was between 40–50ft long, made (if possible) from North American pitch pine. It was mounted in a mast case or tabernacle on deck, and its bottom was curved and shod with iron. This meant that when the forestay tackle was released the mast could be lowered to the deck. There was a tall top mast mounted forward of the main mast, which was usually about the same length as the lower spar. Stumpie barges were those without top masts. The top sail could be set independently of the main sail and was stowed aloft. Its height made it especially useful in docks, or off built-up or wooded shores. The combined height of the two masts required a substantial amount of standing rigging, including a running back stay from the top of the top mast, which was set up via a tackle on the windward side to brace the mast against the wind pressure on the topsail. The two sails, the foresail and the mizzen were all sewn from heavy canvas and 'tanned' with various recipes which included such ingredients as red ochre and fish oil which help preserve them from rot. Modern barge sails have a similar colour but are cut from an artificial fibre called Duradon.

Forward of the main mast, there is a foresail which is hoisted on the forestay and sheeted to another horse running across the deck behind the fore hatch. Ropes known as bowlines, attached to the port and starboard shrouds, are passed through an eye on the leach of this sail to help stop it flopping to leeward. The bowline has to be released each time the barge tacks and it is important not to let it go too soon. This allows the foresail to exert maximum leverage in getting the barges' head through the wind. There is usually a forestay sail which was hoisted on the fore topmast stay. This was a light weather sail. Right aft there was a smaller spritsail. This varied in size; the earlier barges had a tiny one which helped relieve some of the strain on the steering, while later ones had a more useful size. Large coastal barges nicknamed 'mulies' have a larger gaff rigged mizzen. Among the surviving barges, the *Hydrogen* and the *Thalatta* are both good examples of the mulie rig. Barges on longer routes were fitted with a bowsprit on which a jib and a jib top sail could be set. A bowsprit is a nuisance in dock and the barges' bowsprit was pivoted near its heel so that it hoisted up out of the way. Boomie barges were ketch rigged. They could not stow their top sails aloft like the spritties because their gaffs were lowered to the deck when furled. They often carried triangular top sails on both masts and often had a fixed bowsprit. Some also carried one or two square top sails.

Like pleasure wherries, there were barge yachts and these were often featured in the yachting magazines between about 1890 and 1930. They came in a wide range of sizes, from the little gaff-rigged yacht which has a model in the Science Museum, to the clipper-bowed *Thoma II* which had a proper spritsail rig. Some owners took them on long-distance cruises. The *Esnia*, which was built at Rochester in 1910, was narrower in the beam than a commercial barge, and made cruises to Spain. Her professional skipper described her 'as dry as a Pussyfoot and as stiff as a church'. Commercial barges were also bought for conversion into yachts. A.P. Herbert's novel *The Singing Swan* (1968) was a fictional account of such a venture. The barges' roomy holds also made them popular for conversion into house boats.

7

SAILING BARGES OF THE SOUTH COAST OF ENGLAND

There were several different types of sailing barge along the South Coast from the North Foreland down to Dorset. Distinctive barges were found at Rye, on the Sussex Ouse, on the Arun, around the Solent and possibly on the Adur. The majority were inland craft with basic sail plans. Those working on the Solent were mainly small ketch-rigged coastal vessels. Thames barges, especially the boomies, were also very common all along this coast.

For much of its length, this stretch of coast was dominated by steep shingle beaches and/or chalk cliffs. These petered out in the great stretches of water and low-lying land from Chichester Harbour through to the Solent and on to Poole Harbour. Where there were rivers, they were exploited for navigation from early times. The Arun was improved in the sixteenth century. The inland Wey, which had sailing barges and connected with the Thames, was opened to Guildford in 1653 and on to Godalming in 1671, while the Itchen, connecting Southampton water with Winchester, was opened up for barge traffic in 1710.

Yet the main campaign for improvements and extensions to these rivers had to wait until the late eighteenth and early nineteenth centuries. 1787 saw the opening up of the Arun, from its tidal limit 12 miles to Newbridge. In 1791, the Sussex Ouse was improved from Lewes for another 12 miles inland. The Royal Military Canal, which was linked to the Eastern Rother, opened in 1806, and in 1807 the Adur's navigation was extended by 14 miles. The most ambitious scheme was the Wey and Arun Canal opened in 1816 – a 15-mile link between the two rivers. This was part of a through route to Portsmouth which ran from the Arun on a second canal to Chichester Harbour and from thence on to Portsmouth, to provide a safe inland route between the capital and the most important naval base. Aside from the large ports of Portsmouth, Southampton and Poole, there were many small ports and quays along the Hampshire, Dorset and Wight coasts that received freights by sailing barge.

Agricultural produce from inland was a common cargo for all these waterways. It was stimulated not only by the needs of London, but also by the growing demands of the Royal Navy which had to feed the increasing number of sailors, especially in the wars with France

A gaff-rigged swimmie barge pictured in the Solent in the early nineteenth century. Presumably, like the *Teazer* of 1800, she was bringing a cargo from the Thames.

between 1793 and 1815. Coal, timber, sand and stone were also common freights, and, before the building of railways, all kinds of groceries, household and shop goods were also carried. Chalk, as a raw material for cement, was an important freight on the Ouse, the Adur and the Arun, and the finished product was also shipped out by barge from the cement works. The Phoenix Iron Works at Lewes brought in iron, steel and coal by barge into the twentieth century. Clay from Poole and limestone for building from Portland were also carried in barges well into that century.

From the 1840s railways gradually took over much of the freight of the inland barges. The London–Portsmouth through service closed in 1847. The Ouse above Lewes closed in 1868, and the Arun above its tidal limit closed in 1888. Barges continued to work on the lower reaches of these waterways and around Rye until about 1935. Their later work tended to be confined to single bulk cargoes such as chalk, sand or shingle. As these barges wore out, they were not replaced. The coastals continued to thrive. Thames sailing barges, mainly owned by large London firms, had taken over many of the freights from the local fleets of brigs and schooners by the end of the nineteenth century. An early example of a coastal barge passage was found in the Southampton records: on 18 July 1800, the master of the barge sloop *Teazer* of 137 tons burthen reported at Southampton that part of his cargo of wheat from London had been damaged on the passage (*Hampson, 1973: 43*).

Shipyards such as Harveys at Littlehampton turned from building square riggers to ketch-rigged boomie barges. They built thirty-five of them between 1862 and1919. J. & T. Smith of Rye (who had a reputation for building sailing trawlers) also built ten boomie barges between 1888 and 1913 (*Benham & Finch, 1983: appendix*). Their last was

The *Melisssa,* one of the steel barges built at Southampton for Goldsmiths, is undergoing a complete rebuild at Pin Mill near Ipswich.

the *Martinet* of 1912 – the last boomie to trade under ketch rig. Leather extolled the qualities of two boomies built at Poole by J. Allan & Sons, who were mainly yacht builders – the *Princess May* of 1891 and the *Alexandra* of 1894 – which had a fine sheer and deep seaworthy hulls (*Leather, 1984: 148*). Steel barges, which were nicknamed 'ironpots', were built by Fay & Co. at Southampton. In 1898 Fays built an initial eight of these ironpots for E. and J.W. Goldsmith of Grays, Essex. This firm were innovators because they had their barges built of steel in standard designs with interchangeable gear. This octet were all large, 198-ton barges. They were built with round bilges which made them sail well off the wind, but poor to windward. They were not popular with their crews because their metal hulls produced large amounts of condensation in the cabins (*Benham, 1951: 157*). Goldsmith's *Decima* is still sailing and the *Melissa* (1899) is being rebuilt for sailing. Samuel White & Co. of Cowes, which was an offshoot of the Kentish White family of barge builders, built a few composite barges with iron frames and wooden planking.

Some spritsail barges were owned in South Coast ports. Crundalls of Dover had a series of large barges, starting with the *Envoy* in 1895, built to carry cement. They were required for a contract to supply the builders of the extension of Dover harbour. This outer wall was built from thousands of pre-cast concrete blocks. Their other barges included *Sepoy, Savoy* and *Convoy.* The latter was still trading as a motor barge in the 1960s. In the same way, two shipbroking firms at Weymouth (Richard Cox and H.J. Sanson) bought boomie barges at various times in the late nineteenth century, chiefly to handle Portland stone from the local quarries. By 1903 there were some ten barges registered at Weymouth (*Childs, 1998: 8*).

The boomie *Mountsfield* at Strand Quay, Rye, with a local barge alongside, about 1900. (P. Ferguson)

There were another six boomies owned in Littlehampton, eight at Rye, two at Shoreham and one at Arundel (*Benham and Finch: appendix*).

Most of the trade carried under sail to and from the South Coast ports in the late nineteenth and early twentieth century was in the larger spritties and mulies, and later by barges with auxiliary engines. Barge owners with large fleets such as Goldsmiths or the London & Rochester Trading Co. were in the tramping business and sought cargoes wherever they were offered. This meant frequent passages along the South Coast. A representative passage might be cattle food from London Docks to Newport, Isle of Wight, and then light to load clay at Poole for a return trip to the Thames. The L&RTC's *Cabby* of 1928 (still sailing though under new ownership) often undertook this trip in the 1930s, and the *Will Everard* was still working similar freights between 1954 and 1964 (*O'Donnell, 2001: 26*). Down-Channel passages could be long and hazardous, especially during the winter months, because barges had to sail into the prevailing wind with their attendant swells and pass round projecting headlands with their own tidal races.

The Rye barges have been recorded in more detail than those of the Ouse, Adur and Arun. They had just gone out of use in the mid-1930s when the local historian Leopold Vidler set down their history, dimensions and usage. At about the same time, the lines and construction of the barge *Water Lily* were taken and drawn out. In 1823, a barge-like medieval vessel ship was discovered on Romney Marshes in the old bed of the River Rother. It was clinker built in oak, with a flat bottom and double-ended, and measured 63ft 8in in overall length by 15ft beam. It had similar proportions to those of the Humber keel and the Mersey flat, and it was probably a coastal trader (*Carr, 1951: 65*). Town records for Rye recorded a payment to Miles the lighterman for carrying timber as early as 1531. The *Water*

Rother barge *W Body* upstream at Smallhythe in 1924.

Lily, which was still being used to gather shingle for road making in the 1930s, was considered a typical Rye barge. She was long, narrow and shallow – 55ft in overall length by only 12ft 3in beam and 3ft depth in the hold. This provided a cargo capacity of around 20–25 tons. The hull was carvel built and double-ended with the stern more tapered than the bow. There was a very slight sheer, a flat bottom and a rounded bilge. The hull was built up on a keel, closely spaced frames clamped by a keelson and covered by ceiling planks. There were short decks forward and aft, and there were heavy deck beams at each end of the hold which were supported by heavy knees. The forward deck beam also had a tabernacle for holding the 30ft mast. Below the decks, there was a cabin with two berths and a stove, while the aft space was used for storage (*Vidler, 1935: 383*).

For propulsion, there was a lugsail on an 18ft yard. This sail was dressed with red ochre and fish oil. Like other 'tanned' barge sails, a new sail had to be allowed to stretch and to get the stiffening out of the new canvas. There were also tow lines and quants for times when the barge could not be sailed. There was a small tender which was sculled with a single oar over the stern. There was an anchor but no windlass. This was important for barges going out into the mouth of the river to collect shingle. The barges also carried barrows, horses, planks

The *Primrose* discharging shingle dug at Tillingham probably in the 1920s or '30s. Note the number of boards carried to allow the crew to barrow the shingle.

and shovels for digging and loading cargoes (*Vidler, 1935: 388*). According to oral memories, there were about twenty barges working in the 1860s, and barges occasionally made voyages across to France in the summer with cargoes of hops. Between 1872 and 1875, four iron barges were built by the Rother Ironworks at Rye (*Vidler, 1935: 288–92*). The *Primrose*, launched in 1880, was the last barge to be built, She was constructed with diagonal planking which was usually only used for lifeboats and naval service craft. She survived as a hulk into the 1990s and was salvaged in 1992 and taken for permanent undercover preservation at the Shipwreck Heritage Centre in Hastings.

Much less is known about the sailing barges of the River Ouse. They were carvel built, double-ended and 47ft long overall. The impression from the much reproduced photograph of an Ouse barge under sail in the 1920s is that they were broader in the beam than the Rye or the Arun barges (*Carr, 1951: fig. 23*). However, those that proceeded up the locks above Lewes must have been less than 13ft 3in beam to fit through the locks. The hull had more sheer than the Rye barges and the single open hold had low coamings and hatch covers. It had a tanned spritsail on a light mast about 20–25ft high which had no rigging. The sprit was a light pole lashed close to the base of the mast and there was also a second

The hold of the *Primrose* looking towards the bow as she is preserved at the Shipwreck Heritage Centre, Hastings.

A busy scene, with three Thames barges on the River Ouse in centre of Lewes during the inter-war years. (D.R. Macgregor)

Arun sailing barges carried a fore sail and were built with two different types of transom. (E.W.

light pole as a form of gaff along the top of the sail. This was a most unusual arrangement, and as it was also reproduced in an early nineteenth-century view of Lewes it must have been the customary rig (*Bouquet 1972: 41*).

At Newhaven at the mouth of the Ouse there were also yawl-rigged boulder boats which went out to local beaches to collect flint pebbles for shipment to the Staffordshire Potteries. There were also boulder boats working at the entrance to Rye harbour (*Collard 1997: 79*). They appear to have been clinker-built converted fishing boats and not barges (*Simper 1997: 110*). The Adur barges are poorly documented. The locks were 75ft by 12ft 6in, which implied that they were longer and narrower than their neighbours. They had a cargo capacity of between 50–100 tons and were sprit rigged. There appear to have been no photographs taken of them. The English Impressionist Philip Wilson Steer painted three sand barges at the mouth of the Adur in 1926 (held in the collection of the Williamson Art Gallery, Birkenhead). Although the painting is vague and atmospheric, one of the barges looks as if it is rigged with a standing gaff.

Arun barges were different again and within this relatively small fleet there were marked differences as well. They were carvel built, and judging by the surviving motor barge they were chine built with little sheer. They had either a pointed stern or a transom stern. They measured between 40 and 70ft long. The locks on the Arun Navigation and the Wey and Arun Canal restricted their beam to 12ft. Fully loaded, they could carry between 20 and 40 tons. They had

The 1947 *Arun* motor barge at the Boat Museum, Ellesmere Port, preserved the narrow shape and build of the earlier sailing barges. The barge to the right is the last dumb barge from the River Wey. Her predecessors carried spritsails similar to the Arun barges.

Dr. to the

Chichester, Arundel, Petworth & Midhurst
BARGE COMPANY.

N. B. THE BARGES load every WEDNESDAY and SATURDAY, at RANDELLS' WHARF, *Queenhithe, London*, and deliver Goods to the above and all intermediate Places without delby,

The extraordinary two-masted barge depicted on the Chichester, Arundel, Petworth & Midhurst Barge Company's letterhead from the 1840s. (P.A.L.Vine)

E.W. Cooke's lively engraving of a Cowes ketch entering harbour shows that the rig was well established by 1828, but the bows are more bluff than in later barges.

A more stylised depiction from the same era showed a lug sail barge at Southampton with a cargo of barrels under a canvas tarpaulin in the open hold.

A loaded barge with the wind scarcely filling her sails goes down the River Itchen with the tide around 1900.

open holds with four hold beams and no side decks beyond the covering board, and there was a small raised deck forward. If there was a cabin, it was a cramped, low space below the helmsman's position. They were variously rigged with square, lug or spritsails. For tidal work, there were sweeps, and for upriver and on the canal they carried quants and tow ropes. The mast was stepped well aft. Perhaps the sprit rig was the most typical, or perhaps we take it as typical because of the two classic photographs of the barges *No.64* and *Reliance* which appeared in Vine's standard work (*Vine, 1986: plates 38 and 46*). The light mast was stepped well aft in a tabernacle next to a beam in the hold and was supported by two shrouds and a forestay. The latter could be slacked off to lower the mast by a small winch at the fore end of the hold. The sprit appeared to have been lashed to the mast and also supported by a standing lift and vangs, in a similar fashion to the larger Thames barge sprit. On *No.64* at least, there also appears to have been a short boom on the foot of the sail. The sail had two brails, and some barges also used to set a foresail. The letterhead of the Chichester, Arundel, Petworth and Midhurst Barge Company, which ran twice weekly packet service to London into the 1840s, showed a barge with raised bulwarks at the bow and stern, coamings and hatch covers and two equal-sized spritsails and a foresail. Presumably this was an accurate portrayal of one of their fleet. The larger barges that were particular to the Wey also carried spritsails.

No Arun sailing barges have survived; there were only two left, including *No.64*, on the canal by the 1880s (*Vine, 1986: 51*). The tidal barges seem to have been working up until about 1914. Chalk for reinforcing the banks of the river was carried in the River Authority's dumb barge after the Second World War. It was replaced in 1947 by a motor barge built by Hillyards at Littlehampton. It measures 58ft long by 10ft 10in beam, and seems to have been built along the lines of the earlier sailing barges: chine built with a sharp bow without any flare, closely spaced frames and two side keelsons instead of a centre one. It worked until 1965, when it became a

A busy scene around 1900 at the Coal Quay, Newport, Isle of Wight, with ketches and lug-rigged barges loaded with coal.

landing pontoon for yachts, and then was saved for preservation by the Wey & Arun Canal Society. When no suitable berth could be found locally, it was transported (probably mistakenly) to the Boat Museum, Ellesmere Port. It is there today, lying neglected and out of context.

Although the barges of the Solent and the adjacent harbours are usually lumped together, according to Peter Ferguson, retired editor of *Topsail*, the journal of the Society for Sailing Barge Research, there were many variations according to the builders of the barges and their locality (*Ferguson, 2006*). Bosham and Emsworth had shipbuilding firms that built barges. William Foster, who moved from Southwick on the Thames to Emsworth in 1861, built barges and larger sailing vessels for local owners. The *Fortis* of 1904 was the last barge built at Emsworth for William Farne, who owned a waterfront mill at Birdham on Chichester harbour (*Leather, 1984: 143*).

John Crampton was a Portsmouth coal merchant who had contracts to suppy the Navy with coal. He had a fleet of coastal colliers and some barges. The latter were used to deliver bunkers to warships at anchor. He had his own repair yard at Portsmouth. His shipwrights occasionally built new barges, including the 34-ton *Emerald* in 1877. She and three others they launched were miniature boomies with chine-built hulls and lee boards. This quartet was unlike most of the other local barges which had well-rounded bilges and no lee boards. The average size of all the local barges was between 20 and 30 tons. The majority seemed to have been built at Cowes. These ketches were being used at least as the early 1800s. The *Bee* (which was still trading 100 years later) was built in 1801 and was reputed to have victualled some of the warships that took part in the Battle of Trafalgar in 1805. She was also known to have carried oak to the Beaulieu River for building warships at Buckler's Hard. She was carvel built

A Solent ketch making its way up Fareham Creek at the head of Portsmouth harbour under fore sails and mizzen in 1910.

with an overall length of 50ft, a breadth (beam overall) of 14ft 6in and 6ft depth of hold. The 20-ton *Arrow*, which was built at Cowes in 1875, had similar dimensions and lines. Leather described the latter as having 'a slack sheer, rounded bow profile, plumb but shapely transom and well-formed body sections' and these had 'considerable resemblance to the hulls of local fishing boats which were fast and weatherly little craft on limited draught' (*Leather, 1984: 148*). If E.W. Cooke's 1828 engraving of one of these ketches is to be believed they were certainly capable of sailing well in a bit of a blow.

These Solent ketches were strongly built with closely spaced oak frames and thick carvel planking. The deck layout seems to have been fairly standard, with a large hatch with low coamings. Some had a set of curved wooden hatch covers, others (one suspects for coal haulage only) had no covers. Some like the *Bee* and the *Arrow* had proper built-up rails, and others had no more than a raised section about 6in high round the bow and about a 2in kicking board along the sides. There was an anchor windlass forward, and access to the chain locker and stores in the bow seems to have been via the forward hold bulkhead rather than through a hatch in the deck. There was a cabin aft for the crew of two, and this was entered by means of a central companionway. The iron tiller (not a wooden one as in so many other types of barge) with a wooden hand grip projected over the top of this. There was a wooden water barrel lashed to the deck.

Solent barges were noted for their large sail area. They had long gaffs on both masts, tall top masts to carry a triangular top sail and running bowsprits, and two head sails. Both the foresail and the main sail were sheeted down to iron horses on the deck. The mizzen sail was sheeted to the stern post. There were two winches bolted on either side of the mast for the throat and peak halliards of the main sail. Each mast went down to the keelson as there was no need to

A Solent barge tied up at Portsmouth Dockyard in 1917. This humble sailing barge was tied up astern of a battleship with a bucket dredger on the other side of the railway line down to the harbour station. (Marine & Cannon Books)

lower the masts, and both were supported by two or three shrouds. A small boat was normally towed aft. A standing gaff and no boom, like a hoy, was another variant of the local barges' rig. A good example was the *Myrtle* of 45 tons built at Emsworth in 1898, and owned by Fraser and Co. of Portsmouth. This arrangement was also seen on the open-decked sloops that specialised in carrying sand up to the Ballast Quay at Fareham (*Langley, 2005: 38 and 64*).

A photograph of Newport Coal Quay early in the twentieth century shows a smaller type of barge. The three examples in the picture were double-ended and about 30–35ft long with open holds. They were lug rigged and the mast and yard was lowered on top of the hold. They were fitted with a substantial rubbing strake which suggests that they were used to go along side steamers at anchor to supply them with bunkers. Cowes attracted a large number of yachts in the summer including many steam yachts. These would have needed coal supplies.

It is difficult to estimate the number of barges plying the Solent because while some were recorded in the Shipping Registers, others were not. An educated guess based on the *Mercantile Navy List* suggests that there were probably about fifty in 1900. A few barges plied under sail up to the Second World War. The *Tally Ho* of 1912 seems to have been the last to carry sails and was only converted into a motor barge in 1950. There were several other ex-sailing barges plying under motor to and from Newport in the 1950s. These included the *Fox* of 1898 and the Thames barge *Celtic* of 1903 (*Langley, 2005: 128–9*). Unfortunately, none of the Solent ketch barges have survived. There used to be the remains of several, including the *Diamond*, in Velder Creek off Portsmouth harbour, but even these last pathetic relics have been destroyed (*Ferguson, 2006*).

8

BARGES OF DEVON AND CORNWALL

Several distinct types of sailing barge were to be found along the south-west peninsula of England. In the nineteenth century there were also substantial fleets of ketches and schooners in ports such as Salcombe and Appledore, which worked both in coastal and deep sea trades. For example, Salcombe was a noted port for building and owning fast schooners employed in the fresh fruit trade from the Mediterranean and the Azores.

The southern coasts of the counties of Devon and Cornwall had the advantage in water transport of a series of estuaries from the Exe down to the Helford River, which run a long way inland. Some had deep water channels which allowed seagoing vessels to get upriver at high tide. The northern coast was mainly rock bound, but the Camel, the Taw and the Torridge provided water access to the market towns of Wadebridge, Bideford and Barnstaple. The local sailing barges, especially those trading coastwise, had to be seaworthy enough to cope with the tremendous Atlantic swells that were strongest at the mouth of the Channel and made worse at times by the spring and autumn south-easterly gales.

In Devon and Cornwall there was less call for the building of barge canals, and besides, the local topography with steep hills closing in the river valleys made their engineering difficult. The most important routes from the point of view of sailing barge history were the Exeter Canal, and the Stover and Hackney Canals. Exeter had been a major port with foreign trade since the Middle Ages, and access for seagoing vessels was extended up to the city by a canal opened in 1563. This extended another 2 miles lower down the estuary in 1825. The other two were short canals leading off the upper Teign estuary to provide access to china clay workings and were opened in 1743 and 1825 respectively. There were also a number of tub boat canals which were built with inclined planes rather than locks. For example, the Bude Canal, opened in 1823, was a barge canal for the first few miles and then branched out into a 35-mile system with inclined planes and wheeled tub boats instead of conventional barges.

As neither county had any coal mines, coal was a vital cargo. This was shipped in mainly from the South Wales coalfields or alternatively from Lancashire via Runcorn on the Mersey. This was the transhipment place for china clay shipped from the South West. It made a useful

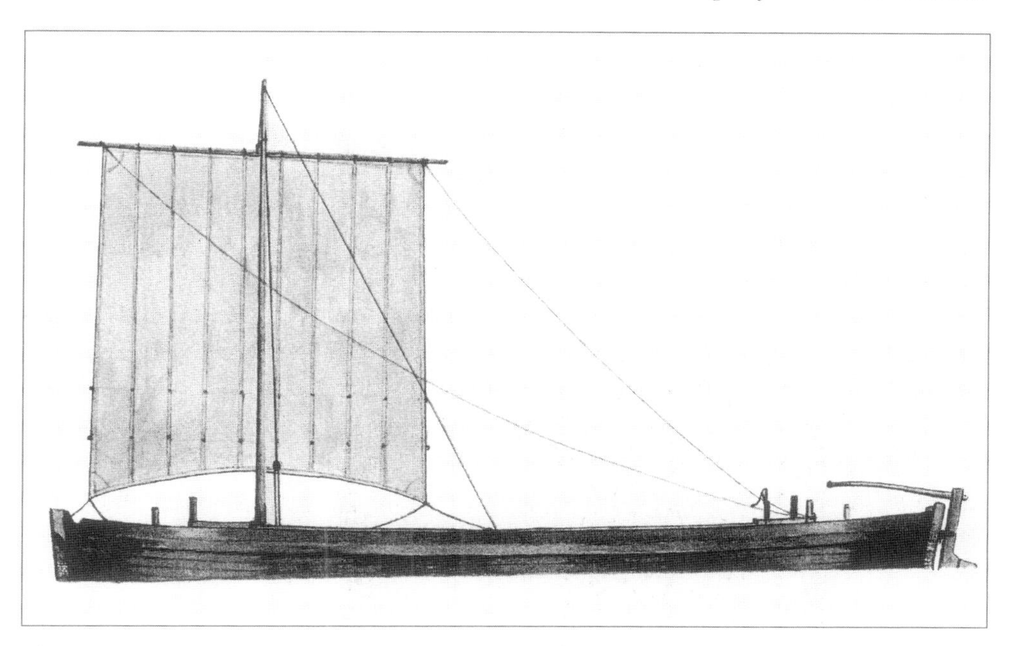

The Teign barges were of the simplest design but eminently fitted for their task. (E.W. Paget-Tomlinson)

back cargo for local schooners. As there was deep water in many of the estuary creeks much of the coal could be delivered direct without transhipment into barges. On the other hand, barges handled most of two other vital commodities – limestone and sea sand. Much of the land was acidic and was deemed to require large quantities of lime or sea sand with a high lime content to neutralise the inherent acidity. The aforementioned Bude Canal was built largely to cope with this trade. Similarly, the survival of thirty-two lime kilns or kiln sites, for calcining the limestone on the Fal and its tributaries, and fifteen on the Tamar, is evidence of its importance (*Ratcliffe, 1997: appendix B, and Booker, 1971: 60–68*).

Although tin, copper, lead and silver had been mined in small quantities as far back as the Roman occupation, there was a boom in metal ore extraction in the early to mid-nineteenth century. Steam-pumping engines enabled miners to dig ever deeper mines in the quest for the richest veins of ore. This industry was gradually eclipsed by cheaper sources from overseas in the late nineteenth century. China clay was the other mineral that was special to the region and this was shipped out in large tonnages for the pottery industry and for paper-making.

The estuaries with distinct types of barge were the Exe, the Teign, the Tamar and the Fal on the South Coast, and the Camel, Taw and Torridge on the north one. In the eighteenth century there was work for sailing lighters bringing up coal to Exeter from seagoing vessels in the lower estuary. In 1715, there were 125 lighter movements and by 1794 this had increased to 306 (*Duffy etc. [eds], 1994: 71*). There were local barges with the distinct function of fetching limestone from the quarry on the coast at Babbacombe, near Torquay. The Davy family were the leading firm of lime burners on the Exe in the late eighteenth and early nineteenth centuries. Their business expanded into farming, selling coal and repairing and

The ketch *Good Intent*, built in 1790 at Plymouth and still trading in the Bristol Channel in the 1930s, was a coasting version of the Tamar barge. (A.A. Hurst Collection/David Clement)

building new ships and barges. Daniel Davy (1799–1874), the second generation in the business, kept a memoranda book which provides much detail on both the lime burning and shipbuilding parts of the business. By 1822, he was operating six stone barges as well as shallower sailing lighters which could trans-ship the stone up to lime kilns on the shallow sections of the estuary. With an average capacity of about 45 tons, Davy's barges made 552 voyages for stone which produced 37,505 hogsheads of lime (*Ponsford, 1988: xv*). Daniel Davy built the barge *Eclipse* in 1819. She measured 56ft 1in overall length, 18ft breadth and half an inch off 8ft depth of hold. She was built with narrower decks than earlier barges, and was sloop rigged (*Ponsford, 1988: 8*). The rig of a later barge photographed at Topsham about 1900 showed a curved stem, counter stern with a short bowsprit with two head sails, a short top mast and a large main sail. The 'stone boats' had the depth of coastal sailing vessels and one of Davy's rival boats, the *Ceres* of 1818, was lengthened and re-rigged as a schooner. These deep draught barges meant that Davy also needed smaller sailing lighters. The *Lucy* had two accomplices – the *Increase* and the *Tiger* – which measured 40ft by 15ft 9in by 2ft 6in. They were rigged with lugsails and had open holds (*Ponsford, 1988: xxv*). The barge *Charlotte*, a later sailing barge built at Topsham by Holmans – a late nineteenth-century firm of shipbuilders – was a ketch-rigged boomie complete with leeboards. She was owned at Portsmouth and regularly carried coal from Portsmouth to Christchurch, Dorset.

The port of Teignmouth was the shipment port for ball clay and granite, which were carried down from either rail sidings at Newton Abbot or the Stover and Hackney Canals. There were seventeen barges plying on the estuary in 1795, with another ten on the Stover Canal (*Trump, 1986: 23*). The barges were 50ft long overall, 14ft in the beam and 3ft 6in depth of hold. They were carvel built with a transom stern, a flat bottom without a projecting keel

The Tamar barge *Shamrock*, laid up at Plymouth in 1974 before her restoration. This photograph gives a good view of the shape of the hull.

and curved sides. They were decked fore and aft, with the latter providing shelter for the crew of two. The tops of the frames projected above the deck to form the stanchions of a low rail, and there were low hatch coamings to the open hold. The rig was a simple square sail which was used on the tidal reaches of the Teign. Otherwise the barge was propelled by poles or towing from the banks of the canals (*Greenhill, 1997: 133*). The cargo of clay, which was usually about 25 tons, was delivered to ships at mooring buoys in Teignmouth harbour. The trip, with unloading, usually took a day, and there might be a return cargo of coal, timber or sand. Some barges returned empty because their owners (who were mainly the operators of the clay pits) did not want the clay contaminated with coal dust. Barges were built locally either at Teigngrace or Teignmouth, and by the early 1900s were operated by three companies. In 1904, the steam tug *Kestrel* arrived on the estuary, and from then on most barge movements took place under tow rather than under sail (*Trump, 1986: 63–64*). The Stover barges were given names, while those on the Hackney Canal were allotted numbers. By 1931, there were sixteen unrigged barges left, but all were old and in disrepair, and all traffic finally finished in 1942 (*Paget-Tomlinson, 2005: 152*).

The broad beam, wide transom stern, the Plymouth gallows, the cabin companion way and the large hatch of the *Shamrock*.

The next type of distinctive barge was based around the Tamar estuary; here there was plenty of work for the great naval dockyard at Devonport and in transporting limestone, coal and minerals to and from upriver quays. Tamar barges were split between those that worked only inside the estuary and were not registered, and those that went outside. Both types were of similar tonnage, and a barge could change from being an inside barge to an outside one according to demand. For example, the *Shamrock* of 1899 (now preserved at Cotehele) was built for inside work but became an outside barge after 1919. However, sailing trials with the restored *Shamrock* on trips to Fowey and the Dart confirmed that the shallow draft Tamar barges were at a distinct disadvantage, especially when going to windward compared with the deeper coasting schooners and ketches (*Allington, 2006: 11–12*). The outside ones were to be found at ports along the Devon and Cornish coasts. A photograph taken at Salcombe around 1908 (which is impossible to reproduce) showed the Plymouth-built barges *JNR*, *Emma*, *Phoenix* and *Yealm* all moored together at Salcombe (*Murch and Fairweather, 1982*: 21). The *Good Intent* which had been built at Plymouth as far back as 1790 was a regular trader between Cardiff and the Somerset port of Bridgwater into the 1930s.

A typical Tamar barge was carvel built with a flat bottom and well-rounded bilges. The proportions of hull made for a beamy and shallow draft vessel with average dimensions around 50ft in length by 16ft beam and 5ft depth of hold, and this gave them a cargo capacity of around 50 tons. The *Shamrock* was one of the largest, measuring 58ft long by 18ft 10in beam and 5ft 4in depth of hold. The smallest ones could be as little as 30ft long. The hull had a 12in- deep keel which assisted their windward performance. When built, the *Shamrock* had two drop keels which must have enhanced her windward performance. This type of moveable keel

Many of the ketches built on the Tamar had sufficiently flat bottoms to sit upright in mud berths. The *Garlandstone*, built at Calstock on the Tamar in 1909, is berthed at Morwellham Quay, the Tamar mining port.

Much of the Fal barges' trade was taken away by steamers or the railways, but in this case a Truro barge in about 1912 has gained a tow from the excursion steamer *New Resolute*.

was common among North American coasters but never caught on for British barges and coasters. Her drop keels were removed in 1919 when the river trade had dried up, and she had to have a load line and safety certificate for outside work. There were at least 130 registered barges built in the nineteenth century, and, as only a few of the inside barges were registered, the total was probably double that. Given the fact that many of these stout craft worked for fifty years or more, this total demonstrates the extent of the traffic on the Tamar in the nineteenth century.

Tamar barges had slightly curved stems, not much sheer and broad transom sterns. They had sharp lines compared with other types of barge with a good run aft, though not as fine as the Cornish versions. On deck they had a large single hatch with low coamings and hatch covers, low rails, or none at all in some cases. There was a substantial cast iron winch just forward of the mast, and the 'Plymouth gallows' was a particular feature aft of the tiller. This was partly a fastening point for the main sheet tackle, and partly to be used as mooring bitts for the stern ropes. There was a small forecastle and a larger stern cabin for the crew of two or three. When the barges were fitted with engines from the 1920s, the aft cabin became the engine room and the crew had to cram into the small cabin in the bows instead.

Most barges were single-masted cutters, and there were some ketches as well – among them the *Shamrock*. Their masts were often set up in a tabernacle on deck so that they could be lowered. The standing rigging usually comprised two shrouds to each side and a forestay. They had a large gaff main sail with the boom projecting over the stern, and most seem to have had a sliding bowsprit. Most of the inside barges had pole masts, while many of the outside barges carried a top mast (*Greenhill, 1999: 144*). But, like bargemen elsewhere, the Tamar crews had not only to sail their boats but had to pole, tow or kedge them as well. They

Four Fal barges and a steam lighter receiving cargo from the steamer *St Cuthbert* in Falmouth Roads in 1904. (Captain G. Hogg)

became very knowledgeable about the characteristics of particular reaches of the river and highly experienced in handling their barges.

Perhaps the most important source of propulsion were the tides which ran fiercely well up the Tamar. In June 1985, the *Shamrock* underwent a river trial by making a trip from her base at Cotehele up to the former mining port of Morwellham Quay. Her volunteer crew used long sweeps and poles using the force of the flood tide and, when the tide ceased to serve, the ship's boat was used as a tug or a kedge anchor laid out and the barge would be drawn up to it by hauling in the cable. Sailing was tried and was not successful on the day, and the sails would only have been of use when the wind was right aft (*Allington, 2006: 13–19*).

The *Shamrock* was rescued after a long career as a stone carrier in 1974, fully restored to sailing condition, and is preserved at Cotehele Quay by the National Trust. The extensive quays, warehouses and lime kilns have all been restored, which provide her original commercial context. Elsewhere, the barge *Lynher* was salvaged in the 1990s by a private owner and restored, but is now laid up near Plymouth facing an uncertain future. The coasting ketch *Garlandstone* was built at Calstock on the Tamar in 1909 and has been restored at Morwellham Quay. Although longer and deeper than the local barges, she was built with flat floor amidships to allow her to sit upright at low tide.

The Fal estuary reached as far inland as the county town and port of Truro, and its barges were similar in function and design to their Tamar neighbours. They were much fewer in number because there was no major industrial complex equivalent to Devonport Dockyard. Nevertheless, the recent survey of the estuary identified about seventy quays serving local mines, water mills, foundries and even stately homes (*Ratcliffe, 1997: appendix B*). Many local

A bow view of the same scene as on p.103, with three more barges on the port side of the *St Cuthbert*. (Captain G. Hogg)

firms such as brewers and mill owners ran their own barges. Carne's brewery at Falmouth had two barges – the *Graham* and the *Topsy* – which delivered barrels of beer mainly to Truro for inland distribution. A Mr Collins who ran a water mill and a coal business at the head of the remote Gillan Creek had the 30-ton *Industry*. There were other specialised barges as well. The main types were the barges that dredged up sand, those that lightered cargoes from ships anchored in Falmouth Roads, and outside barges that collected stone (mainly for road making) from coastal quarries such as those at Porthoustock, further west of the Fal. In addition, there was a mid-nineteenth century packet service for goods and passengers, with three barges sailing on a daily rotation between Truro and Falmouth. This was still running in 1853, but must have given way to steamers and then to the railway. There were also lug-rigged lighters and tonnage boats carrying farm produce to market in the nineteenth century. The latter were only 18ft-long open boats (*Argall, 1978: 165–6*).

The typical Fal barge was generally narrower and deeper than the Tamar barge. This made them better performers under sail. The *Mystery* was built at Truro in 1885. She measured 55ft 7in in overall length, 17ft 2in beam and 6ft 6in depth of hold. This made her 10in narrower and 14in deeper than the *Shamrock*. Her hull had much finer lines as well. While this meant a reduction in cargo space, her windward performance and general seaworthiness must have been enhanced, and given the big Atlantic swell that affects the sea immediately off the entrance of the Fal, this was no bad thing. There were other detailed differences; the stem was more curved, the transom was smaller and higher and sloped in a similar way to those of the Cornish luggers. The hull was strongly built with a keel 12in deep, double frames and

Loading sand on a barge at the entrance to the Camel about 1900. The size and general rig and layout was very similar to the barges of the Taw and the Torridge. (Captain G. Hogg)

a keelson which was also 12in in depth with inner and outer layers of planking. On deck, the hatch had smaller dimensions and there were higher bulwarks, including a higher section around the stern. There was a store area in the bow and a cabin at the stern for the crew of two or three, and there was a similar type of cast iron winch/windlass in the bow for anchor work and cargo handling.

The rig was similar to the Tamar barges, but yet again with detailed differences. The mast was fixed on the keelson and so could not be lowered. There were three shrouds and a top mast back stay instead of two, and the lower part of the leading edge of the main sail (the luff) was laced around the mast, while the upper part was secured by the more usual wooden hoops. It is also interesting to compare the sail area of the *Mystery* with that of the *Shamrock*. Although the *Shamrock* had an extra mast, she only carried 1,081 sq. ft of canvas, while the *Mystery* carried 1,641. The *Mystery*'s extra sail area of 560 sq. ft was mainly accounted for by a main sail which was almost double the size of the *Shamrock*'s. Her top sail had an area of 306 sq. ft. These would have been much more of a handful in heavy weather. By dividing the sail area between masts, the *Shamrock*'s crew could, if necessary, drop her main sail, and sail on the forestay sail and mizzen.

But the *Mystery*, as with some other later survivors, may not have been altogether typical. She clearly represented the high point in the development of the Fal barge, and she was one of the last to trade under sail. Photographs of other barges show a much simpler rig and in some cases a hull form closer to the Tamar version. For example, the *Mary*, which was built in 1875 by the most respected builder on the Fal, H.E. Stephens of Devoran,

The partially restored but unknown Taw and Torridge gravel barge at St Osyth, Essex. Note the low rails, the hatch coamings and the tabernacle for the mast.

measured 49ft 4in by 17ft 6in by 5ft 7in. These dimensions made her beamier and shallower than the *Mystery* and yet she was regularly coasting between the Fal and the Tamar. As with other types of barge, only a few survived long enough to be recorded, and afterwards these plans have been taken as absolutely typical of the whole species. This may not be the case because every builder and every owner had slightly different ideas about their design.

Transport by barge on the Camel estuary of north Cornwall goes back at least until the early seventeenth century. In 1626, twenty-six bargemen were listed as living in the villages of Egloshayle and St Breock. The main ports were Padstow, at the mouth of the Camel, and the important market town of Wadebridge, which was situated at the lowest crossing point about 7 miles inland. Barges were used to lighten ships bound for Wadebridge with imported timber, coal, slate and limestone, and to ship out iron and copper ore from local mines. Latterly, barges were engaged in gathering sand from the outer estuary for transport to Padstow. John Bartlett lists twenty-two barges plying the Camel in the nineteenth and early twentieth centuries. A high proportion were built elsewhere, including one built at Freckleton on the Lancashire Ribble and a de-rigged boomie barge, the *Genesta*, whose wreck is still visible (*Bartlett, 1996: 47*). Most were sloop rigged and, judging by the photograph of one of the later sand barges, they were not dissimilar to the sand barges found further up the coast on the Taw and Torridge estuaries. There was also a larger type of very broad-beamed barge which was rigged as a schooner but without a bowsprit. These are only known from a number of photographs taken around the start of the twentieth century. Unfortunately there seems to be no precise details about their dimensions or build.

The sand barges of the combined estuary of the rivers Taw and Torridge are much better known and some worked as motor vessels until the 1960s. They started as general-purpose vessels used for lighterage, transporting clay to the thriving potteries at Barnstaple and Bideford. Both ports could trace their origins back to the Middle Ages. As the railways took away their other trade, the barges were left with gravel from the ridges in the estuary. Much of this was shipped coastwise in larger vessels to Avonmouth or Cardiff for major new dock works.

They were rugged little vessels. The last one built along sailing barge lines was the *JJRP*, launched at Appledore in 1923. Her owner, Captain John Pile, insisted she was built to the scantlings of a vessel twice her size. She measured 37ft in overall length, by 13ft 5in beam and was 5ft 4in from the deck to the keel. Her maximum load was 27 tons. She had thick oak frames which supported larch outer planking nearly 3in thick, which in turn was backed by internal planking of almost 2in thickness (*Grant and Hughes, 1975: 43*). The *JJRP* and her sisters had a fairly bluff bow, flat bottom, a hard turn of the bilge and a good run aft. On deck there was a single hatch with hatch boards and tarpaulins which were always well battened down when returning loaded. There was a cabin in the bow for the crew. They could shelter and cook there after they had shovelled up to 30 tons of gravel and before the tide refloated their barge. The aft space was a store and later an engine room. The *JJRP* was fitted with a 10hp Widdop semi-diesel within about two years of her launch, which served her all the time up to her retirement in 1961. The sail plan was simple, just a main sail and foresail, and the main sail gaff was set at a lower angle than the Tamar barges. The pole mast was set in a tabernacle for shooting the bridges at Bideford or Barnstaple, and was supported by two shrouds and a back stay.

The *JJRP* was acquired for private restoration after finishing in the gravel trade, but was badly damaged by fire and sunk. In 1974, she was raised by the North Devon Museum Trust with a view to preserving her. Unfortunately, this voluntary body could not raise the necessary cash (there was no Heritage Lottery Fund then) and she had to be abandoned. There are the rotting remains of a barge close to shore at East-of-the-Water, Bideford, and I presume this must be the poor old *JJRP*. Another of these north Devon barges was taken to Essex as a private preservation project, and today lies neglected and unfinished at a boatyard at St Osyth.

9

SEVERN TROWS

The upper Bristol Channel and the rivers that drain into it were water highways to a wide and distant hinterland to the east, west and north. The River Severn is the biggest and longest river in the British Isles, and was navigable for much of its length up to Pool Quay, near Welshpool in North Wales. As it and its tributaries drain an area of heavy rainfall, its levels can rise dramatically by as much as 25ft. Particular stretches can silt up or shoal. Long stretches can be dry in summer and ice over in winter. The tidal section has the highest tidal rise and fall in the whole of the British Isles. In the 16-mile section between Sharpness and Framilode the tide can run as much as 7 miles an hour. In other words, it was a thoroughly hostile environment for water transport. Nevertheless, sailing barges sailed these waters from an early date. The Barlands Farm boat, which dates from about AD 200, is evidence of early sailing barge traffic in the upper Bristol Channel. The Severn was known as a commercial waterway in the Middle Ages, and by the sixteenth century it was busy with trows carrying cargoes such as coal from the East Shropshire mines down to the salt works at Droitwich, and corn from the fertile Vale of Evesham to market in Bristol. These kinds of bulk traffic increased and diversified in the seventeenth century and by the eighteenth century the Severn served a growing number of industries along its banks. The Darby's pioneer iron works at Coalbrookdale is just one example.

The Severn was left unimproved until the late eighteenth century, when locks and tow paths were built northwards from Diglis (just below Worcester). These helped to maintain water levels in its higher reaches. In 1818, the stretch from Gloucester to Worcester was tackled, and in 1827 a ship canal was opened from Sharpness to Gloucester. Its tributaries, especially the Warwickshire Avon, were feeders, as were other rivers that flowed into the Bristol Channel. The River Wye and its tributary, the Lugg, flow into the Bristol Channel to the west of the Severn. They shared many of the Severn's navigational problems, but after improvements made in the late seventeenth century, they provided another 70 miles of navigation to Hereford and Leominster. The Bristol Avon connected the port of Bristol with the sea. From 1712 barges could sail up to Bath, and in 1812 it was connected with

Two trows sailing inland from Gloucester in the Bucks' view of that city in 1734.

the new Kennet and Avon Canal to create a through-route from London to Bristol. The Parrett, the other major commercial river, carried barges to Bridgwater and from thence via the River Tone and various canals to Taunton and the inland areas of the county of Somerset. There were other smaller rivers and numerous creeks (known as 'pills') and small ports such as Lydney along its margins.

The extent of the trade even before 'the improvement era' has been recently documented in David Hussey's study of the river and coastal trade of Bristol between 1680 and 1730. Possibly the Severn as a whole reached its peak in the middle of the eighteenth century. George Perry's description of the river's traffic, published in 1758, listed 210 owners possessing 376 vessels between Gloucester and the limit of navigation (*Trinder, 2005: 144*). The construction of canals in the West Midlands in the later eighteenth and early nineteenth centuries took away traffic from the upper stretches of the river. Iron founders in particular were often frustrated by the delays caused by drought or bad weather and used canal narrow boats instead of trows. By 1840, there were 3,412 shipments by canal from Gloucester (the hub port of the Severn) and 954 by the river (*Trinder, 2005: 113*). The upper Severn above Bewdley (although it had been improved with the building locks) declined first. By 1830, only a few trows worked above Shrewsbury and by 1850 there were only two trows a week sailing beyond Ironbridge (*Trinder, 2005: 119–121*). New railways – such as the Severn Valley Railway, opened in 1861 – finished off the last Upper Severn trows. The very last one carried a cargo of bricks in 1895.

The word 'trow', as a description of a vessel, was in use by 1411. It seems to have been derived from the word for a trough or hollow vessel. This idea of a hollow vessel is neatly encapsulated in a Bronze Age log boat on show at the Rowley House Museum, Shrewsbury. Its flat bottom, deep sides with sheer at the bow, and the curved swim bow (rather like the

A trow on the Upper Severn with cargo of timber from Bucks' view of Shrewsbury in 1732.

The 'frigate' type of trow with a high stern and tall mast off Worcester porcelain works in 1757. The boat to its right is a Severn passenger-carrying wherry.

Two of the last Upper Severn trows at the Ludcroft Warehouse, Ironbridge. This Gothic building was built to house products of the Coalbrookdale Foundry awaiting shipment. It now has an extensive display about trows and the trade on the Severn. (Ironbridge Gorge Museum Trust)

Thames lighters of the seventeenth century) demonstrate that this could have been an early cargo carrier on the upper reaches of the Severn (though paddled rather than sailed). In the last 300 years, there were two types of trow: the better-known downriver and coasting barge that survived under sail into the middle of the twentieth century, and the upriver versions which had died out by 1900.

The latter was the older type and was built in a completely different way to the other. Graham Farr, who wrote the first (and still authoritative) paper on Severn trows, considered that they probably originated from Viking vessels (*Farr, 1946: 66–95*). The most recent accounts of the origin of trows have benefited from the extensive discoveries of medieval shipwrecks on the continental coast of the North Sea since the end of the Second World War. There has also been the revealing excavation of an Upper Severn trow at Lydney in 1992. This trow's construction had closer affinities with that of the North German cogs of the twelfth century than any earlier Viking boats (*Greenhill, 1997: 183 and Green, 1999: 52*). The main similarity was the way the hull was built with a flat carvel bottom and clinker sides. The trow may also be related to other flat-bottomed barges with carvel bottoms and clinker sides, such as the Bridgwater flatner or the fleet trow of Chesil Bank, Dorset (*Green, 1999: 60–1*). Neither of these types of boat (with the exception of the fishing flatner) carried sails, hence their exclusion from this survey.

George Perry's description of the Severn, published in 1758, mentioned not only trows carrying 60 tons but also smaller barges, called frigates, which had a cargo capacity of 40 tons.

Above and below: This Avon stone barge (*see detail, below*) was making its way downstream under sail and using a pair of sweeps. (Bristol Industrial Museum)

No one is quite sure how the term arose except that the frigate is a smaller type of sailing warship. Trows could load 60 tons or more, but this figure varied according to the depth of the river. So, for example, in 1761 the trow *Coney Green* was described as capable of carrying 60 tons on a 4ft draught, and 30 on a 3ft draught. Recent research among the inventories of vessel owners has shown that many had sets of vessels of different sizes. This enabled them to trade along the capricious river with the maximum amount of flexibility. In 1723, for example, Thomas Andrews of Bridgnorth had a frigate called the *Cunney* worth £18, a barge named *Hannah* worth £20, and a share in a trow, the *Loving Brother*, worth £60 (*Trinder, 2005: 22*). There were also smaller tenders. Some were described as tow boats, cock or cockell boats. They had various uses: taking soundings, towing when the wind failed, transporting the team of bow haulers or horses from one side of the river, and transhipping cargoes on shallow stretches. As late as 1881, the 65-ton barge *William* was sold at Jackfield near Ironbridge, along with a boat carrying 16 tons (*Trinder, 2005: 28*). The records also tend to indicate that the owners on the Upper Severn only described vessels as trows if they traded on the wider tideway below Gloucester to Bristol, Chepstow etc. Barges for them were the river craft – more suited to the higher parts of the river. A magnificent blue and white punch jug in the Rowley House Museum, Shrewsbury, bears this out. It is inscribed: 'Success to the town and trade of Shrewsbury, Richard Eaves, barge owner, 1812.' But instead of a painting of a barge, it has a Chinese junk! The terminology appears to have been loose, because on the other hand, Edward Owen owned 'a great trow, a middle trow and a little trow', according to his will of 1732 (*Trinder, 2005: 23*).

Until the excavation of the remains of the trow abandoned at Lydney near the entrance to the dock, all the evidence for the design of the Upper Severn trow or barge had to be deduced from prints or photographs. The excavation revealed a 40ft section of a hull that measured about 72ft in overall length with a beam of 15ft 6in and 4ft 6in overall depth from the deck to the bottom of the hull. It was originally constructed with a flat carvel bottom and turn of the bilge and clinker topsides, bow and stern. The planking was fastened to 4in-thick oak frames. There was no keel so that the bottom of the hull would not snag when it grounded. The carvel bottom and bilge plank were of thick Scotch pine to withstand the wear of constant grounding. Carvel build, with its edge-joined planks and caulking, also survives better when kept wet. Drying out tends to make it leak, and so it was ideal for the bottom. On the other hand, clinker building, with its overlapping planks, is lighter than carvel, withstands drying out better and is probably easier to repair. The combination of the two produced a barge hull that could cope with the navigational problems of the Severn. Dendrochronological dating has concluded that the oak used to build the trow was probably felled in 1823. The trow was rebuilt on two later occasions when it received additional carvel planking, a keel and possibly a change of rig to allow it to sail on the Severn estuary (*Williams, 1992: 16*).

The Lydney trow seems to have been typical of the upriver trow, judging from the evidence of contemporary photographs. There was a distinctive convex bow and a transom in the shape of two inverted 'D's. There was an open hold with decks fore and aft. There was a forecastle cabin for the crew and a master's cabin aft, often with square ports cut through the transom stern. The mast was just forward of midships and carried square sails. The Bucks' view of Gloucester of 1734 showed a number of trows with a main mast with a square main and top sail like a Humber keel, plus a foresail on a bowsprit and a lateen mizzen. There were other smaller ones – possibly frigates – with a single mast with one or

The smack-rigged trow *Superb* was built at Bower's Yard, Shrewsbury, as an Upper Severn trow in 1826. She had been rebuilt and re-rigged for estuary work by the 1890s. (Bristol Industrial Museum)

two sails. Hancock's engraving of the Worcester Porcelain Works of 1757 showed another trow with the two-masted rig and an elaborate raised stern similar to that of a small warship. Perhaps this kind of stern accounted for the nickname frigate. Hancock also drew a smaller passenger wherry with a single mast, four rowers, and hoops for a canvas tilt to protect the passengers in bad weather. Henry Nash's *History of Worcestershire* of 1781 has a number of engravings of the river with trows with a single mast with top sails.

The main mast had a separate top mast abaft, and sat on the keelson in a tabernacle, and could be lowered with a windlass to pass under fixed bridges. There was also a short bowsprit to anchor the top mast stay. The combined height of the masts on a 56ft-long trow would have been over 60ft, with the main sail over 30ft and the top sail 18ft deep. These measurements are based on Richard Barker's plan (*Green, 1999: 65*). Such a towering sail plan would have helped where the river flowed through narrow, wooded gorges, such as that at Ironbridge. There were four shrouds supporting the mast which had ratlines. This implied that the crew had to climb aloft to furl the sails, rather than the yard being lowered to the deck as with the Humber keel. It must be emphasised that this was essentially a running rig and that the opportunity to tack in this fast-flowing river was limited. Downriver passages were greatly assisted by the current, while upriver ones were often undertaken by teams of men or horses hauling the trow from the river bank, or by the crew rowing the trow or rowing it from the cockell boat.

Photographs of the later upriver trows show a simpler rig with just a main sail. The stone barges of the Bristol River Avon also had the simpler rig and were still plying the Avon

The little *Industry* – all of 38 tons – was built at Chepstow in 1871, and was involved in the stone trade from Lancaut quarry on the Wye. She had an open hold and bulwarks. Under a magnifying glass, a women can seen sitting aft – possibly the skipper's wife. (Bristol Industrial Museum)

Gorge well into the era of photography. Trows on the Warwickshire Avon, judging by a print of Bidford Bridge by Samuel Ireland, had the same shallow hull form, a large single sail and were steered by steering oar instead of a rudder. The Wye trows were similar and lasted until about 1876. There is an excellent scale model of a Wye trow in the Monmouth Museum.

While the Upper Severn trow was in sharp decline, there was an increasing demand for carrying bulk cargoes on the lower estuary and along the coast. The coal and limestone trade had been carried in trows across the Bristol Channel between the Somerset and north Devon ports and South Wales since the seventeenth century (*Farr, 1959: 380*). But the opening of major docks at Gloucester, Sheerness and Avonmouth, and the rise of South Wales coal as the prime source of fuel for steamers, stimulated the demand for a different kind of trow. This was a carvel-built coaster which was built in a conventional way with a double set of frames. There were even a few iron-hulled trows. The flat bottom, without a projecting keel and the characteristic inverted 'D'-shaped stern, were retained. It was also noticeable that many were built or rebuilt with a concave rather convex profile to their stems, which made them look more like other types of coasting smack or ketch. The hulls had similar proportions but they gradually increased in overall size. For example, the *Frederica*, built at Gloucester in 1869, was a ketch measuring 73ft 2in by 19ft 2in by 6ft 2in and with a tonnage of 62. The *Sabrina,* another ketch-rigged trow, built at Gloucester in 1893, measured 85ft 2in by 20ft 2in by 8ft with a gross tonnage of 116. Some of the older trows

The long-lasting *Jonadab* with a rebuilt stem and bulwark resembles a West Country coasting ketch. She carries three jibs and a large top sail, and most of her sails appear to be tanned. (Bristol Industrial Museum)

were rebuilt; the *Stroud Packet*, built on the tributary Stroudwater at Brimscombe Port in 1823, was taken in hand and 'boxed' in 1876 to dimensions of 73ft 2in by 15ft 6in by 6ft 7in with a tonnage of 62. Her depth was almost doubled.

Although the size might have increased, the shape of the hull (except for the depth) was similar to the earlier ones. The entrance at the bow was fairly bluff and there was a short run aft. Later, some trows like the *Norah*, built down channel at Bridgwater in 1868, had a more hollow entrance and run. Some trows, such as the *Alma* of 1854, were equipped with a detachable keel to assist their windward performance. Later trows such as the *Norah* were built with a proper keel as well as bilge keels. All the same, as Greenhill pointed out:

> the hull form was not suited to sailing. It was evolved to maximise cargo capacity in a given length, draught and beam. Such are the tides of the Severn estuary and the inner Bristol Channel that much of the work of these vessels comprised tidal drifting, the sails being used to provide steerage way and control. (*Greenhill, 1997; 184*)

The estuary trow perpetuated the open hold of their predecessors and were known as 'open-moulded' trows. The short foredeck accommodated a windlass and a cargo winch with forecastle for the crew of two below. The aft equivalent housed the master's cabin, which was also blessed with a skylight to relieve the gloom below. The hold was framed by three or four hefty deck beams to provide the necessary structural strength. An open hold was a great advantage to a trow carrying coal in bulk. The cargo could be tipped into the hold straight

The mighty *Emperor* of 1906 drying her sails at the stone quay near St Mary Radcliffe church, Bristol, some time before she lost her sails in 1920. She was as a flush-decked trow with a counter stern. (Bristol Industrial Museum)

This panoramic view of the River Wye at Llandogo shows its rocky hazards and the local trow *George and Mary* of 1851 (rebuilt in 1878). She was left on the gravel shoal between voyages and eventually rotted away there after her owner's death in 1913.

The *Spry* has the typical inverted 'D'-shape of transom. She also has quite a fine run aft. Different builders built very different hulls while conforming to the general features of trows.

from railway wagons with the minimal amount of trimming. At its destination the coal could be discharged rapidly with a grab crane. These open-moulded trows had iron stanchions along each side of the hold on which canvas screens could be rigged in bad weather to keep out the waves. For more perishable freights, tarpaulins could be rigged over the hold. Box trows had built-up hatch coamings instead of side cloths. The final development was the flush-decked trow which had the distinctive hull of the trow, but with the small hatches and raised bulwark of any other type of sailing coaster. Several of the survivors working in the twentieth century had been built as open-moulded trows and were later converted into the flush-decked version. The *Jonadab*, which was named by a presumably evangelical owner after a minor character of the Old Testament, had been built at Newport in 1848 as an open-moulded trow. Colin Green thought it possible that she was first rigged with a square main sail and a spritsail on the mizzen (*Green, 1999: 68*). In 1895 she was rebuilt as a flush-decked ketch with bulwarks. After she was rebuilt, she traded as far away as southern Ireland and the South Coast of England.

The later trows were either rigged as smacks or ketches, and their standing and running rigging was similar to other sailing barges with these rigs. Some carried a long bowsprit which could carry one or two jibs, and in some trows, such as the *Jonadab*, this spar was long enough to be able to carry three jibs. The forestay sail was often fitted with a boom across its foot and the top sail was a large square-headed canvas with a jack yard at its head. These can be seen on the photographs of the *Superb*, the *Industry* and *Jonadab*. Some trows had tanned sails, others did not, and some had a mixture depending on the age of the canvas.

The bow of the *Spry*, seen here at Blist's Hill Museum before her restoration, has a much finer entrance with some hollow below the waterline.

The *Spry*, fullly restored and afloat at the Bristol International Festival of the Sea in 1996.

There was also a type of trow which was special to the salt trade from Droitwich. These 'wich barges' had a maximum length of 60ft and a beam of 14ft 6in to fit the locks on the Droitwich Canal. They had more sheer than the typical trow and an elliptical transom similar to that on some Thames barges. But they retained the open hold and the side cloths. They carried a foresail and jib and a main sail with a long hoist on a 50ft (or so) pole mast. Their paint scheme was more colourful than the trows which were usually tarred black. Their upper planking at the bow and on the stern quarters was painted red, and the stern with the name and port were picked out in yellow on a red and green background, with the lower transom painted white. Between 1812 and 1895 some fifty-five of these barges are known to have been built (*Green, 1999: 89*), and they carried salt to Gloucester , Bristol, Lydney and to some of the fishing ports of Somerset and Devon. Rail transport deprived them of most of their cargo by the end of the nineteenth century, and the Droitwich Canal was closed in 1916. The surviving barges were transferred into the general lighterage trade, and most of them lie abandoned and partially buried at Purton on the south shore of the Severn.

There were lots of sailing trows working mainly in the coal and stone trades up to around 1920. Edmund Eglinton's recollections give an insight into the life and trades of trows, such as the *Palace* and the *Irene*, which delivered stone for sea defences on the beaches of north Somerset (*Eglinton, 1982: 1–30*). In the years between the two world wars trows were motorised or cut down to dumb barges, and by 1939 only three retained their sails. Besides these there were about 100 in use as motor or dumb barges. By 1959, there were only eight left carrying cargo (*Farr, 1959: 386*). Most of these were condemned over the next few years, but rather than breaking up their tough ancient hulls they were put ashore at Purton or Lydney to help stop erosion. It was a different outcome for the *Spry*. She was launched at

The Kennet & Avon stone barge *Harriet* ended up on the marsh at Purton. She has sunk considerably since this picture was taken in 1987 but her name can still be seen carved on her stern. (Dr Frank Howard)

Chepstow in 1894 as an open-moulded trow of 41 tons with a smack rig. In 1913, she was changed to a ketch rig and continued trading under sail until 1936. She became a dumb barge, and from the 1950s she was used as a store and workshop at Diglis Basin, Worcester. She lay there derelict for some time until she was rescued by the Upper Severn Navigation Trust in 1983. She was the last trow to remain in good enough condition to be restored. She was taken by road to the Blist's Hill Museum at Ironbridge. Over the course of the next ten years she was completely rebuilt retaining only one original deck beam with her tonnage measurements carved into it (*Johnson, 1995*). In 1996, she was one of the star vessels at the Bristol International Festival of the Sea. That year, she also sailed on a calm summer's day on the Bristol Channel, and in 1997 she went on show again at Bristol and Gloucester before being moved back to Blist's Hill, where she sits safely in her shed – the last of the Severn trows.

10

MERSEY FLATS

Liverpool grew from a coastal haven in the early seventeenth century into a bustling Atlantic trading centre by the early eighteenth century. By the middle of the next century it had grown to become the second port of the kingdom after London, and an international giant with worldwide connections. The humble sailing barge, the Mersey flat, was a small but vital cog in the intricate mechanism of distributing cargoes to and from Liverpool, either inland or along the adjacent coasts.

It is probable that the flats were direct descendants of the sixteenth and seventeenth century barks that carried on Liverpool's coastal and Irish trade. These barks had an average cargo capacity of 20 tons and were rigged with one or two square sails. Some later seventeenth-century barks may have been converted to fore and aft rig with a gaff main sail and two head sails. Such vessels were depicted in the first view of Liverpool which was painted in 1680 and again in later views, and most notably in the Bucks' view of 1728.

There was growing amount of lighterage work between anchorages and the quays at Liverpool. The Hoyle Lake was the outer anchorage on the main approach channel to the Mersey. This was where deeply laden ships would discharge part of their cargo to reduce their draught for the final run into the Mersey. Most ships then anchored off the quays at Liverpool while their cargoes were lightered ashore. Lightering cargoes was standard practice in many ports of the time, including London, where deep-sea ships moored in the Pool opposite the Customs House. Liverpool's anchorage could be dangerous because of the fast current and the high tidal range. The Sloyne, off the south bank of the river, provided a more sheltered anchorage which also needed flats to ferry cargoes. This situation changed with the opening of the first enclosed dock at Liverpool in 1715, and this was followed by the building of a chain of enclosed docks which allowed vessels to stay afloat and discharge at quays whatever the state of the tide.

But this was not the end for the flat. There was another beginning for them in 1720, when three Acts were passed to authorise the opening up to navigation of the rivers Mersey (beyond Warrington), Irwell, Weaver and Douglas. The works consisted of digging new channels to cut off the worst meanders and building locks. The first to open was the River

A seagoing, gaff-rigged flat from Bucks' 1728 view of Liverpool. Note the high stern inherited from its predecessors. A painting of the Mersey at Warrington from 1772 shows this continued into the later eighteenth century.

Weaver in 1732, and this allowed flats to carry coal for salt-boiling at Northwich and Winsford (the two centres of the Cheshire salt area), and to deliver the finished product to Liverpool for export abroad and to the British fisheries. The Mersey and Irwell Navigation followed in 1736, and this allowed the passage of cargoes between Liverpool and the growing textile town of Manchester. Then, in 1742, the River Douglas was opened up from the coast to the north of Liverpool, to Wigan with its rich coalfield. In 1757, the insatiable demand for coal led to the building of the first of the new artificial canals. This was the Sankey Canal from the upper Mersey estuary to St Helens and its coal mines. Between 1757 and 1816 a network of wide canals was built in the North West, linking the major industrial towns of Lancashire and Yorkshire to Liverpool, with added connections to London, the Midlands and North Wales via narrow canals. The wide canals were built with locks that could accommodate flats, or more often flat-shaped dumb barges which were towed by horses.

A square-rigged 'inland flat at the Manchester 'Key' of the Mersey & Irwell Navigation in 1742. Note the lug mizzen, a sail dropped on later flats.

The characteristic fan-shaped framing of the bows of a flat. In this case, the *Oakdale* of 1953.

Flats came in different size. The sand flat *Gladys* must have been among the smallest. Note the well-rounded bilge and the large rudder – both typical flat features. She is also similar to the barges that plied the Mawddach estuary.

The term 'flat' seems to have come into use for the sailing barges on the Weaver, and these only had a cargo capacity of 20 tons. The first named flat, the *Concorde*, was built at Miry Lane, Wigan (which still exists), in 1742. She was larger than the weaver flats, possibly because she had to make coastal trips to Liverpool. She measured 45ft along her keelson and probably about 55ft in overall length, 14ft 6in beam and 5ft 4in depth of hold. In later times, flats were built longer, and the standard dimensions were around 63 to 67ft long and 14ft 6in beam. The width remained fairly constant because of the restricted dimensions of many of the inland locks. The depth of hold was between 6ft to 7ft 6in. The coastal flats tended to exceed these dimensions, and the last sailing flat ever built – the *Santa Rosa* of 1906 – measured 74ft 4in by 19ft 6in by 8ft 7in, with a registered tonnage of 93 gross tons. There were wider variations according to the trade. The *Birkenhead* of 1861, which specialised in delivering consignments of gun powder to ships safely anchored in the estuary, was only 11 gross tons

A typical late nineteenth-century flat; note the size of the spars in comparison with the crew of two. The fore stay is a combination of chain and a long iron rod. The boat towed behind was known as a cock boat. (Liverpool Record Office)

(*Paget-Tomlinson, 1962*: *353–355*). At the other end of the scale, the dumb flat *Gowanburn* of 1902 was 164 tons gross and could carry up to 300 tons of bagged salt.

Flats were carvel built and flat bottomed with a round bilge. Some flats, such as James Bolton's 'flatt' of 1782, had a gently rising floor rather than a completely flat bottom (see Chapter Two). The bow tended to be 'apple-cheeked' above the waterline with a slight hollow below it. On the double-ended flats there tended to be a good run as well. Many flats, especially those on the Weaver, had transom sterns and much fuller stern lines. This gave them added cargo capacity but impaired their sailing qualities. On the other hand, flats depended on the fast Mersey tides for much of their propulsion, and were often towed inland by horses or, as on the Weaver, by teams of men who needed large quantities of beer. Double-ended and transom-sterned flats co-existed; there does not seem to have been an evolution from one stern to the other, although it is probably true to say that there were more double-ended examples built after about 1850.

Flats were built with very strong hulls partly because they were designed to take the ground and partly because their large hatches, though important for cargo handling, weakened the upper part of the hull structure. This had to be compensated for in the lower members. The backbone was the keel and the keelson with the floor timbers sandwiched between them. The keelson was a massive single timber or several large timbers scarfed together. In the case of the large jigger (ketch) flat *Eustace Carey* of 1905, the keelson was 2ft 6in deep and 1ft 4in wide.

Mersey flat with a new sail waiting for a swing bridge to open at Waterloo dock, Liverpool, about 1915 – one of the last flats under sail. Note the halliard winch on the tabernacle and the large size of the blocks on the halliard tackles. (Liverpool Record Office)

Flat skippers were adept at sailing the bulky craft in narrow waters. A flat sails out of the Salisbury Dock, Liverpool, about 1900.

The old flat *Chester* was built in 1827, and was still hauling heavy blocks of stone for the rebuilding of Liverpool Docks in 1905. (National Museums Liverpool)

The development of steam barges from 1863 meant that many flats were turned into dumb barges. Here, a steam barge was towing two flats bound for Warrington about 1910.

Scarcity of timber saw some later flats fitted with H-section iron girders as keelsons. There was a curved stem post with a reinforcing deadwood and a straight stern post with a deadwood bolted to each end of the keel. Again, these were large chunks of oak, 9in wide and 11in deep. The cant timbers which formed the shape of the bow were a noted flat feature which was not seen in other sailing barges. Their fan shape has also been seen in the remains of the late eighteenth-century brig *Betsy* which was built at Whitehaven (*Delgado, 1997: 472*), and in an eighteenth-century yacht preserved at the Windermere Steamboat Museum. Perhaps this feature was part of an older shipbuilding tradition particular to north-western England.

Flats were planked with 2 to 3in oak with 4in planks around the turn of the bilge. There was a ceiling in the hold which was usually made of 3in-thick pine. Deck beams measured between 6 and 8in deep and 6 and 7in wide. Later flats had iron hanging and lodging knees instead of wooden ones fashioned from oak crooks. There were a number of flats built of iron, such as the *Decempedes* of 1879. While more expensive to build than a wooden flat, an iron flat could last longer, as the *Decempedes* proved. She was converted to a steam barge and later had a diesel engine, and was not scrapped until 1969. There were also some flats with composite hulls: iron frames and wood planking. The giant *Gowanburn* was one example. Having said that, some wooden flats lasted for more than a century. Of course, they all underwent major rebuilds at roughly 30-year intervals. The *Daresbury* was probably the oldest. She was built by Samuel Edwards at Northwich in 1770, and was just under 50ft long with a cargo capacity of about 67 tons. In 1802, she was lengthened by 8ft and underwent extensive repairs in 1831, and again in about 1864. At the latter date she was converted from a sailing flat into a lifting barge and survived in use on the Weaver until 1956. Her sunken remains are partly visible along with other flat hulks at the old lock at Sutton Weaver.

Ship bunkering was one of the few estuary trades open to sailing flats by the 1890s. Here, the *Elizabeth* has taken on a coal cargo at Bramley Moore Dock, Liverpool, in 1894. (National Museums Liverpool)

Illustrations ranging from the Bucks' 1728 panorama to Donbavand's painting of Warrington of 1772 (in the Warrington Museum) showed earlier flats with a lot of sheer. Even the flat at Manchester Quay, which appeared on Casson & Berry's map of 1741, had much more sheer than her nineteenth-century successors. If these illustrations are accurate (and there is no doubt that they were intended to depict flats), these flats must reflect their origins in the coasting barks of the sixteenth and seventeenth century. The typical nineteenth-century flat did not have nearly as much sheer, and those trading solely inland had none at all. The coasting jigger flats had a raised bow, as can be seen in the painting of the *Petrel* of 1873 and the photograph of the *Eustace Carey* of *1905*. Flats had no bulwarks, but invariably had rails round the steering position aft. These were a safety measure and also provided anchor points for the relieving tackles for the tiller. Like many sailing barges, flats had a large rudder which needed a long tiller to provide the necessary leverage. This long spar could take charge in bad weather, hence the need for the tackles. As an added measure, there were also foot grips fastened to the deck. Coasting flats either rigged a lifeline along side decks or had rails which could be removed in port so they did not get in the way of cargo handling.

The deck was dominated by a fore and a main hatch with the mast stepped between them. They had high coamings and curved hatchboards which were covered with tarpaulins. These wide openings could make flats vulnerable in bad weather. Accidents occurred in the river when the master of a flat neglected to replace the hatchboards and the tarpaulins after leaving a dock or a canal. On 11 July 1857, the flat *Samson* came down from the Weaver with a cargo of salt and with the hatches open. There was a sudden squall and the salt cargo became saturated, and the flat sank off Canning Dock entrance at Liverpool, drowning the mate, the skipper's wife, a

Sailing flats were often built and owned beyond the Mersey. These three flats were based at Fleetwood, Lancashire, around 1900.

niece and nephew. Some of the large coasting flats owned in Runcorn had been converted to topsail schooners in the 1850s and 1860s. The extra canvas and the large hatches, which were far bigger than those of a proper coaster, made them vulnerable in bad weather (*Starkey, 1981: 123–4*). Judging by the reports of lifeboat rescues from flats sailing between the Mersey and the Dee, they were vulnerable even in Liverpool Bay. However, flats sailing this route, and indeed those on the upper Mersey, faced negotiating treacherous and shifting sandbanks. The innate strength of a well-found flat's hull meant that many were salvaged after their stranding.

Right in the bow, there was a massive anchor windlass which was needed because flats often had to anchor to wait for the tide to change. Anchors could also be used to 'spring' a flat in calm weather. This skill is known as 'dredging' or 'kedging' on other barges. It involved a flat drifting with the tide, quickly letting go her lighter (kedge) anchor with just sufficient cable to touch the bottom and momentarily bring her up. She would then swing her head to the flow of the tide, her rudder would be put hard over in the required direction and the anchor would be raised from the bottom. She would then move stern-first with the tide. The whole operation would be repeated as often as necessary. It called for a great deal of skill and co-ordination between the skipper on the tiller and the mate at the windlass. The windlass also carried two smaller winches mounted above the main barrel. One was called the barrel winch and carried 90 fathoms of rope which could lead over the bow via a block on the forestay. This line could then be ferried across to a suitable dockside bollard by the mate sculling the cock boat. Once attached, the flat could then be warped across the dock. Flats which frequently had to lighter cargoes from different ships in different docks had to resort to the barrel winch to move in these confined water spaces.

The jigger flat *Eustace Carey* just after her completion at Clare & Ridgway's yard at Sankey Bridges near Warrington in 1905. Her burnt-out remains are still visible on the shore at Widnes West Bank.

Many sailing flats, after converting to dumb flats, were worked into the 1950s and then disposed of in large numbers. Some were burned, others were buried like the five that filled one of the redundant locks on the Bridgewater Canal at Runcorn. (E.W. Paget-Tomlinson).

The other winch was to raise the mast after it had been lowered. This was worked by a heavy four-sheave tackle on the end of the forestay. Many late nineteenth-century flats did not have lowering masts, unless they worked on the Weaver where there were still several fixed bridges.

There was a store for spare sails, rope etc. in the forecastle. It might also contain a bunk and a stove, and these would be used if a third hand was carried or if the skipper had brought his wife with him. The main cabin was aft below the steering position, and was usually no more than 7ft long and 6ft high. There were two cupboard bunks, fixed benches, a folding table which doubled as the food cupboard door, and a cast iron coal stove. Because many trips were short ones, most flatmen also had a home ashore. Although, some of the Victorian health inspectors inspecting flats' cabins reported damp, dirty and unhealthy conditions, most latter-day flatmen took great pains to the keep their cabins clean, tidy and well-painted (*Stammers, 1993: 159–161*).

Going back on deck, there were a series of substantial timber heads (bitts) for mooring lines and tow ropes. The pump or pumps were possibly unique pieces of equipment. This was because they were made from drilled-out elm trunks. Elm was a very good at resisting rot and these primitive but effective appliances have been found still intact in the wrecks of flats. One pump was located just aft of the main hatch where it also acted as an anchor for the lower main sheet block. Flats were tarred black with the name, port and often the owner's name on the stern and the name alone on each side of the bow. On deck, red and yellow were popular colours for the bitts, rails, windlass and blocks. The coamings might be grained and there were sometimes grained panels on the stem and either side of the bow. The top of the mast was painted white and the owner's colours were painted in bands between the white and varnished portion of the mast. There was usually a brass or copper windvane with a long length of red bunting.

The last survivor, the dumb flat *Mossdale* of 1867 looking well maintained at the Boat Museum, Ellesmere Port. Unfortunately, she has been allowed to deteriorate badly since the photograph was taken in 1977.

The main mast sat on the keelson. It had a rounded heel shod with iron to assist its lowering. It contained a tabernacle which was open on the aft side, and that open side had a pivoting iron 'gate' to hold the mast in place. On deck, the tabernacle had a winch with a barrel on each side of the mast. This was mainly used to help with hoisting the main sail. The spars of a flat were usually of a massive size. The mast was often a single piece of pitch pine of 12in diameter, and the main boom could be as long as 40ft. The gaff was also a long spar and was set at a much more acute angle than on most other barges – about 30 degrees to the mast as against between 40 and 50 degrees on other gaff-rigged barges such as the trow or the Humber sloop. The Norfolk wherry was the only other barge which had such a long gaff set at such an acute angle. The mast was supported by three shrouds on either side of the hull. As usual, these were tensioned by lanyards and deadeyes. What was unusual was that the lower deadeyes could be unhooked from their chain plates, and the reason for this arrangement was probably the occasional need to clear the standing rigging out of the way when loading alongside another vessel. The forestay was the only other piece of standing rigging, and if the mast could be lowered there would be a massive tackle fastened to the stem. If it was a fixed mast then sometimes the forestay was an iron rod.

The running rigging was simple and fitted with tackles to assist the crew to 'rig' the sails. Flatmen always talked of 'rigging' a flat, not setting its sails. The foresail sheet was shackled to a ring on an iron horse fixed across the deck, and there was a bowline that could be cleated to the foremost shroud for hauling the leech of this sail taut. The adjustment of this bowline was quite critical because there was no means of hauling in or releasing the sheet. The main sail was raised by peak and throat halliards. The peak halliards were led via a single block at the top of the mast to an iron ring through which a chain passed. In turn, the chain was attached to the gaff by two strops. The throat halliards were led from a block on the mast to a double tackle. The blocks of these huge wooden affairs were about a foot long. The main sheet ran through three single blocks and was cleated to the top of the pump within handy reach of the helmsman. There was also a topping lift to support and adjust the boom. Sails were allowed to stretch when new, and then tanned with red ochre and fish oil. Flats seemed to manage to sail without leeboards, even when light. However, some flatmen declared they were 'hard mouthed' – they carried too much weather helm.

The earliest inland flats were rigged with square sails and some also carried a top sail and a foresail on a bowsprit. Square sails probably disappeared from the Mersey by the 1750s. The flat at Manchester Quay of 1742 had a small lug mizzen aft which may have been a throwback to older bark rig – assuming it was an accurate depiction. Further north, Brockbanks, the Lancaster shipbuilders, were launching flats at the end of the eighteenth century which had single square sails, for use on the Douglas and the Ribble. As with other kinds of nineteenth-century sailing barge, there were variations in their rig for a small minority. The earliest two-masted flats were rigged as galliots with a square topsail on the main mast, and this rig was later simplified to ketch or jigger rig. Jigger flats often carried small topsails and a jib. Some early nineteenth-century flats registered at Liverpool, which must have been in the coastal trades, were rigged with sliding or lifting bowsprits.

Steam towage was introduced on the Mersey in 1824, and by the end of the nineteenth century most flats had lost their sails and were towed. There was a steamer version of the flat – the Weaver Packet – which was introduced in 1863. Packets took over the Weaver traffic and towed dumb flats as well as carrying their own cargoes. Sailing flats were still to be found at work on the estuary and coastwise. Many of the transatlantic liners took in new coal supplies from flats while at anchor in the river. Other flats were involved in lighterage between docks and factories, and in collecting sand and gravel. There was a small group of flats that were based at Fleetwood in the sand trade and the same port was used by the jigger flats of the United Alkali Co. They sailed mainly between Flint and Fleetwood. By the end of the First World War, there could have been no more than twenty flats under sail and this number rapidly reduced in the next decade. The very last was the *Keskadale*, which was in the Widnes sand trade until about 1945, although most of the time she was towed rather than sailed.

Dumb flats survived for rather longer and two new ones were built in the early 1950s. However, the rapid decline of barge traffic in the 1960s saw their end. Many were burned or buried in out-of-date docks. Today, only two survive intact, and both of these are dumb flats. The *Oakdale*, built in 1953, was built with different, more bluff lines than the traditional flat. She survives as a house boat on the Duddon estuary at Millom. The *Mossdale* of 1867 is more typical and is part of the collection of the Boat Museum at Ellesmere Port. This museum also has two wooden Leeds and Liverpool Canal boats which were shallow draft versions of the flat. Unfortunately none of these large wooden barges have had much attention in recent years. The *Mossdale* now lies sunk, and much of her upper works appear to be rotten. It would be a great shame if this unique barge were to be broken up, and there seems to be little prospect of building a replica sailing flat.

11

BARGES OF WALES, SCOTLAND AND IRELAND

Descriptions of the sailing barges of these three nations have been placed together because their barges were fewer in number and a lot less has been published about them. They shared no common characteristics and they have been placed together purely for ease of reading.

WALES

Wales has an extensive coastline bounded on the east and the south by the Severn estuary and the Bristol Channel, and by the Irish Sea and the Dee estuary to the west and the north. There were navigable rivers and a few canals that provided access to the inland areas. The Welsh sailing barges were Severn trows around the Severn and the Bristol Channel, and Mersey flats to the north. There was also an extensive fleet of deep draught sloops based in many of the small ports, especially those around Cardigan Bay. On the other hand, Wales has been blessed with the discovery of the remains of five barges, dating back to the Barlands Farm boat of the third century (*Delgado, 1997: 254*).

From the late eighteenth century, the ports of the Forest of Dean through to Swansea exported millions of tons of Welsh coal. The local anthracite was particularly good for firing steam boilers and came to be in demand right across the world. Rivers such as the Loughor were used by barges to bring coal for transhipment into larger ships at anchorages and quays in its estuary. The Monmouthshire Canal opened in 1792, the Swansea Canal in 1798 and the Glamorgan Canal in 1799. In addition, a number of shorter waterways which opened in the same period were narrow boat canals, which linked the rich inland coal mines with the ports of Newport, Swansea and Cardiff respectively. Coal-based processing industries such as copper and iron smelting called for imports of ore. The Magor Pill Boat was a medieval sailing barge which was discovered on the mudflats of the Severn Levels in 1994. About 25ft of the clinker-built hull survived. Its timbers were dated to about AD 1200 and it was found

Welsh sloop *Idris* discharging stone (on her starboard side) shows off the deep and shapely hull of her type. Note the bilge keel to protect the bilge planks when she was beached. (National Museums Liverpool)

The Dwyryd sailing barge, excavated at Cwch Talsarnu. The position of the mast is clearly seen abaft the second deck beam. (Owain Roberts)

to be carrying a cargo of iron ore from Glamorgan for processing in the Forest of Dean. It was probably rigged with a single square sail (*Redknap, 1997–8: 23*).

To the west, the Bucks showed a number of square-rigged barges lying off the shipyards at Swansea in 1748. Thomas Rothwell's engravings of the Cambrian Pottery, Swansea, and the Forest copper works at Morriston of 1791, showed a specific type of local lighter with an open hold and transom stern which were being either rowed or poled (*Gibbs and Morris, 1991: 30, 32*). The rivers and creeks serving the coal mines and industries of the ports of Llanelli and Burry Port were used by sloop-rigged barges and smacks. Of those built at Llanelli between 1815 and 1889 the former averaged around 30 tons, and the smacks about half that tonnage (*Craig etc., 2002: 435*). A view of the Burry estuary by Alfred Vickers in 1853 shows a sloop at low tide drying its tanned sails (*Craig etc., 2002: frontispiece*). Lighters of 15 tons capacity were documented carrying coal from Lord Ashburnham's mines at Pembrey for local distribution between 1714 and 1721 (*Matthews, 2004: 57*).

To the west again, the estuaries that served the ports of Carmarthen and Kidwelly may have had sailing barges too. The broad estuary of Milford Haven certainly had sailing barges serving Pembroke, if early nineteenth-century views of Pembroke Castle can be believed. One anonymous lithograph showed an open hold, transom stern spritsail barge, while Turner's view of about 1830 showed a gaff-rigged barge dramatically heeling in a squall. The ports of Cardigan Bay, from Fishguard and Cardigan in the south to Aberdovey and Barmouth in the north, were served by coastal sloops which were the local equivalent of a sailing barge. Their dimensions and hull shape were different from that of the average barge.

The Llyn Peris barge on display at the Electric Mountain Centre, Llanberis, with Owain Roberts, the marine archaeologist who salvaged and reconstructed it.

Their hulls were shorter and deeper, and they did not have the flat floors of barges but a round bilge with bilge keels. They had bluff bows and a good run aft – what was described as 'a cod's head and a mackerel tail'. Comparing them with an average Mersey Flat or a Severn trow shows that these Welsh sloops were smaller and shorter:

Type	Tons	Length	Breadth	Depth of Hold	Length/Breadth Ratio	Breadth/Depth Ratio
Welsh	45.9	45.71ft	16.2 ft	8ft	1:2.82	1: 1.94
Flat	59.9	59.8ft	15.1ft	6.07ft	1:3.89	1:2.52
Trow	72	71.5ft	15.5ft	5.5ft	1:4.6	1:2.8

They were also smaller than the equivalent English and Scottish sloops (*Stammers, 2000: 56*).

The shipowners of these small ports also owned larger ketches, schooners or brigs, but for transporting small tonnages of coal and stone for lime burning to remote beaches and quays, the 30–40 ton sloop, or the even smaller smacks of below 20 tons, were the right size. The small port of Aberporth, for example, owned twenty-five sloops between 1820 and 1840 (*Jenkins, 1982: 85*).

The shallow estuaries of the Dyfi (Dovey), Mawddach and Dwyryd all had their own types of sailing barge. In the case of the latter, the remains of a barge have been excavated and published. Much of the trade was in carrying roofing slates and metal ores down to seagoing ships at the estuary entrances. They also handled timber for export and brought in trans-shipped supplies of coal and other necessaries to the inland towns such as Machynlleth,

Flats were the sailing barges of the coast of North Wales and the Dee estuary which had several busy small ports in the nineteenth century. In about 1910 two flats were loading at Rhyl – a town which is better known today as a seaside resort.

Dolgellau and Cemlyn. There seems to be very little information on the Dyfi barges in spite of an excellent history of Aberdyfi. It is likely that they disappeared after the building of the local railway in 1862, and one of their last jobs was to transport the sleepers and other materials for building the railway. A report in the local newspaper in 1864 recorded the drowning of a local boatman when the foresail of his barge swept him overboard (*Lloyd, 1996: 105*). This implied that the barge was gaff rigged.

We have a better idea of the Mawddach barges that plied to and from Aberffraw/ Barmouth. The accounts of the boatman David Evans for the years 1846–51 and 1856–9 have survived in the National Library of Wales. He carried a great variety of articles including timber, culm (inferior coal for lime burning), coal, flour, rice, oatmeal, iron, lead, soap, treacle, beer, groceries and guano up to inland quays and especially to Dolgellau, via a short canal built in the eighteenth century. His lighter returned with copper, iron and lead ore, paving stones and oak bark (for tanning leather). His business declined with the opening of the railway linking Barmouth and Dolgellau in 1867 (*Lloyd, 1993: 70*). A few local lighters survived long enough to be photographed laid up at Barmouth in the late nineteenth century. They were double-ended carvel barges with a flat bottom and well-rounded bilge. They had an open hold with the mast fitted at the back of a deck beam about a third of the length of the hull from the stem. They were sloop rigged and had a windlass forward and a halyard and cargo winch just forward of the mast. They were about the same size and appearance as the small flat *Gladys*, which is illustrated in the chapter on flats.

Two River Dee barges above the Medieval bridge at Farndon in an engraving of 1817. Note the salmon netting boat on the right of the picture.

The Talsarnu boat was the sole survivor of barges that plied from Talsarnu and later Porthmadog – a new sea port created between 1821 and 1826 – to a series of inland quays, terminating with a short canal to Cemlyn. Lewis identified some forty-two barges ranging between 4.5 and 8.5 tons and discovered some fifteen contemporary prints and paintings showing barges under square, lug and gaff sails, including a ketch. He considered the ketch was artistic licence (*Lewis, 1999: 83–89*). In 1988, the remains of one of the barges were excavated at Cwch Talsarnu. The hull was a combination of clinker sides and carvel bottom, 26ft long by 9ft 6in beam and 3ft depth of hold, with a curved stem and straight stern post. No decks survived; there was a deck beam about a third of the length back from the stem which seems to have had bulkheads for the fore hold, while about 3ft abaft of that is a second beam which carried a socket for the mast (*McElvogue 2003: 44*). Slate was the most important cargo and the opening of the Festiniog Railway between Porthmadog and Blaunaeu Festiniog removed the need for river barging. McElvogue considers that the Cwch Talsarnu barge was abandoned in the 1880s (*McElvogue 2003: 42*).

A similar barge was discovered during the excavations for the tunnel under the River Conwy, but this was destroyed before it could be properly recorded (*Lewis, 1989: 90*). The accounts for a barge built on that river in 1685 showed that it was clinker built and had a square sail and was capable of delivering cargoes of timber to Liverpool (*Williams, 1980: 11*). Two other barges have been excavated from the adjacent lakes of Peris and Padarn. Both were connected with the transport of slate. The one from Llyn Peris was dated to between 1547

These topsail schooners at the Old Quay, Campbelltown in about 1905 could be regarded as gabbarts because they delivered cargoes under sail around the West Coast of Scotland.

An early nineteenth century gabbart having the marine growth burned off her bottom as depicted by John Fleming. (Inverclyde Council –McClean Museum & Art Gallery)

This little sketch of the gabbart *Beaver* appeared in the a 1912 issue of the *Yachting Monthly* . She had been built as a Manx fishing dandy and was later sold for cargo work around the Clyde and thus became a gabbart.

and 1549 and was clinker built, and that from Llyn Padarn had a flat carvel bottom and clinker sides (*McElvogue, 1999: 6–8*). Neither wreck had any evidence that they were sailed, but the design of their hulls would not have ruled out this method of propulsion (*Roberts, 2006: personal communication*) The other Welsh barge was the so-called Mersey flat. This sailing barge should be called 'the North Western Irish Sea flat' because they were extensively built, owned and traded from Conwy all the way up to Whitehaven. In particular the coasts of North Wales and the Dee estuary were major centres for the flat. The only exception was on the River Dee between Chester and Bangor-on-Dee. Square sailed barges of between 12 and 18 tons, and sometimes named as flats, traded in sand, manure, timber, wheat, malt and barley from medieval times down to the mid-nineteenth century. A local survey of Cheshire inland barges of 1795 listed only two – the *Monmouth* and the *True Blue* which were owned at Bangor and Holt respectively. They were crewed by four or five men who used the current and the sail to travel down to Chester, and then bowhauled the barge back. An auction sale advertised in 1838 reported two boats of 12 and 17 tons burthen which plied between Chester and Bangor (*Kavanagh, 1995–6: 59–63*). In 1992, the sunken wreck of a double-ended vessel some 50 to 60ft long was discovered near the castle at Holt. This could have been either a barge or one of the bridge of boats built in the English Civil War to besiege the castle. Unfortunately, the initial discovery does not seem to have been followed up.

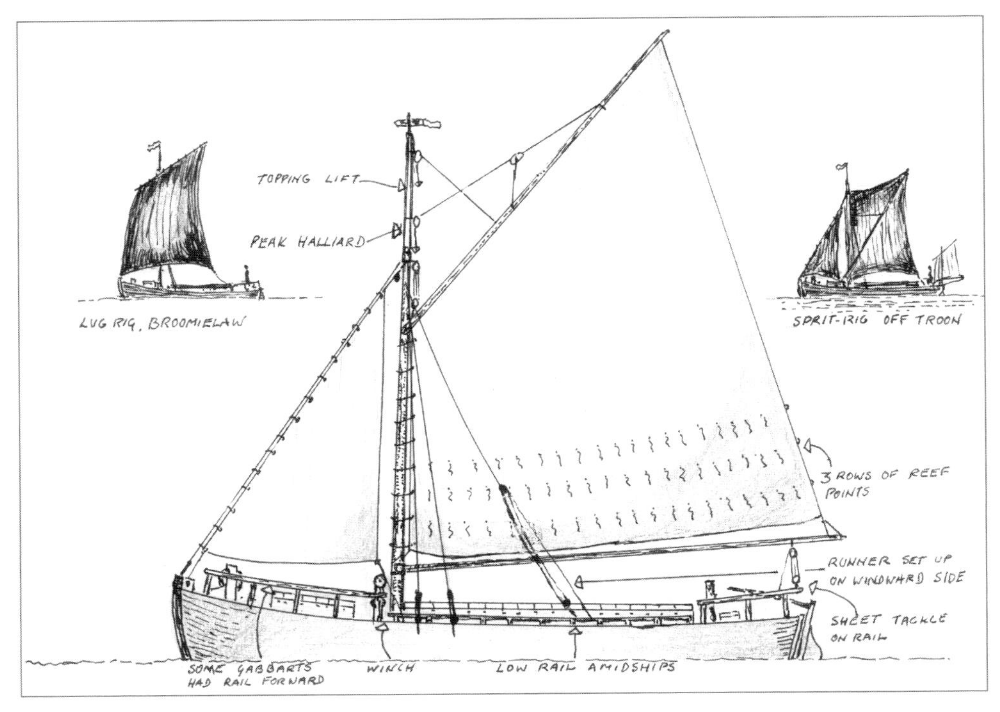

A long time before 1912, there were locally built gabbarts which resembled Mersey flats. This drawing is a synthesis of various illustrations and the two surviving photographs of the Clyde gabbart.

SCOTLAND

While Scotland has long estuaries and two long-distance canals linking its east and west coasts, it was not a sailing barge nation, with one exception. The sailing gabbert was found on the west coast of Scotland centred on the Clyde estuary, going inland on the Forth and Clyde Canal (opened in 1790) and venturing occasionally up to the Western Isles. The Clyde in its natural state has many shallows below Glasgow. The biggest obstacle was the Dambuck Ford, where there could be as little as 2ft of water at low tide. The depths of the river were gradually improved by the careful positioning of training walls of stone which helped to speed up the current, and thereby increase its depth. By 1781, there was a depth of about 14ft over this particular obstacle, and by 1824 it had deepened to 17ft. So, by then it was getting to the kind of depth that allowed deep-sea ships to make the passage, under tow, from the new steam tugs to unloading at Glasgow's quays. But before that, it was a case of lightering goods from big ships at anchor or berthed at Greenock or Port Glasgow, and lighterage was the gabbert's main function. In the eighteenth century, Glasgow's main landing place for cargoes was the Broomielaw, and the regulations laid by the burgh authorities suggest it was very busy with gabberts. They appointed a shoremaster who organised the orderly unloading of cargoes and also ensured that empty gabbarts moved away from the quay quickly. Clause No.3 of these rules promulgated in 1788 stated: 'All vessels loaded with sugar, wine, tobacco, hemp or other weighty cargoes, which cannot be landed with the gabbert's tackle, shall have preference at the crane' (*Renwick, 1913: 284*). So, here is

The iron canal barge *U 66*, which is stored upside down at the Scottish Maritime Museum, Irvine, incorporated the main dimensions of the canal-using gabbarts and probably their shape as well.

a list of cargoes carried by gabberts, and a hint that they carried their own winch and derrick. The Glasgow Directory for 1819 published a tariff of freight rates on the Clyde, and gabberts lightered goods for 4*s* per register ton, or the whole gabbert (of 60 tons upwards) could be hired for 40*s* from Greenock to the anchorage. Once the Clyde had been deepened, and once steam tugs and puffers were well established, sailing gabberts were no longer built and the surviving ones were relegated to secondary jobs such coal carriage.

The definition of the term 'gabbert' is imprecise and does not seem to have covered any one specific type of vessel. The word was probably derived from the French word *gabare* for a lighter or inland river barge, such as those that plied the River Loire. According to the *Oxford English Dictionary*, 'Gabberds' – a variation on the spelling – were first mentioned in 1580. The *Ann Gabbart* of Liverpool was mentioned in the Liverpool Port Book for 1660–61, and at Whitehaven in the 1690s Sir John Lowther's estate manager referred to the coal lighters on the River Liffey at Dublin as 'Gabberds'. The OED does not have these two references, but it has a first Scottish reference for the word in 1775. The term seems to have been applied fairly loosely in the nineteenth century to sloops, smacks and schooners trading in and around the Clyde. In other words, the word described the purpose of the vessel and nothing else. Even the steam powered barges – the famous Clyde puffers – which displaced most of the sailing vessels in the second part of the nineteenth century were sometimes referred to as 'steam gabberts'. The Dutch-built, three-masted schooner the *De Wadden*, which was used for sand cargoes on the Clyde in the 1970s, could probably qualify as a gabbert!

The steam puffer or steam gabbart took over much of the sailing gabbart's freights. The *Kelpie* of 1868 was an early example, and carried a substantial gaff main sail to supplement her steam engine. (Dan McDonald)

While the word gabbert was used loosely for any cargo-carrying coaster, it was also used for a type of sloop-rigged barge within the gabbert clan. Young's *Nautical Dictionary* of 1863 defined a gabbert as, 'a long, narrow, flat vessel or lighter, with a hatchway almost the length of the deck, sometimes fitted with masts which are made so that they may be lowered in passing under bridges.' They were also illustrated in views of the Clyde. The Scottish landscape artist John Fleming (1792–1845) produced a number of views which were published in *Select Views of Glasgow and Environs* in 1828, and these showed gaff-rigged barges on the river. He also painted a gabbert having the marine growth burnt off its hull. This fine and accurate work is in the collection of the McLean Gallery at Greenock. A watercolour of the noted Verreville flint glassworks at Glasgow in about 1836 showed a gabbert that may have been carrying raw materials for glass-making, such as kelp from the outer islands (*Clow, 1952: plate 59*). Bartlett's view of the Broomielaw quay at Glasgow in 1849 showed a host of gabberts – some sloop-rigged and some with lugsails. Sangster's *Picturesque Scotland*, published about 1860, shows a sprit-rigged barge off Troon just to the south of the Clyde estuary. Given that the book's other engravings of Scottish fishing vessels are accurate, this barge must be considered in the same light. They were later associated with Dumbarton, and a Law Report of 1877 specifically referred to them as trading on Leven Water, a tributary river that enters the Clyde at Dumbarton. This was probably one of the few trades open to them after the introduction of the steam puffer in 1856. Samuel Bough (1822–78) painted three gabbarts beached in front of Denny's famous shipbuilding yard at Dumbarton in 1855. This fine work is held behind the scenes of the National Maritime Museum, Greenwich.

A barge with a small sail and little wind on the River Lagan about 1900. (Ulster Folk and Transport Museum)

A painting by William Clark, offered at Sotheby's in 1981 and dated to 1850, shows the Denny shipyard with a gabbert with its mast lowered and a broad white band painted round the hull. There are probably other views of the Clyde that confirm the existence of the gabbert; it is a pity that no-one seems to have discovered a wreck that provide us with more specific details of the gabberts' construction.

But there is evidence in the early nineteenth-century Shipping Registers for Glasgow and from the Scottish canal system. The Glasgow Shipping Registers contain a number of entries for gabberts. Eighteen were registered between 1812 and 1827, so they were not particularly common. There were probably others registered at Greenock or not registered at all because they were confined to inland waters. The Glasgow-registered gabberts ranged in tonnage from 37 to 73 tons, and the smallest measured 42ft 10in long, and the longest 65ft 3in.

Ten were over 60ft long but the average length was just under 54ft. Their beam measurements ranged from 12ft 6in for the *Thomas and Mary,* a former canal lighter, to 18ft for the *Betty*, built at Greenock at 1801, which was clearly intended for coastal usage. The average was 13ft 3in. Their depths of hold ranged from 4ft to 7ft 4in with the average at 4ft 10in. These latter measurements reflected the shallowness of the Clyde, and presumably the deeper gabberts such as the *Lilly* of 1804 concentrated on the lighterage work to and from Greenock and Port Glasgow. Incidentally, the *Lilly* was owned by the Trustees of the Clyde Shipping Co., which was the first to introduce steam towage, and by 1856 the *Lilly* and the other gabberts owned by the company had been converted into dumb barges (*Anon., 1957: 30*).

All the registered gabberts were carvel built and some entries specified that they had a flat bottom. Half were built with round sterns and half with transoms. Eight were built in the Dumbarton area, four at Greenock, three at Old Monkland on the Forth and Clyde Canal

A Lagan barge at the Sand Quay, Belfast, with the rather stiffly posed crew (or is it father and son?). There is an air of neglect about the barge. Note the characteristic low rail, the mast lying on the hatch covers and the cast iron pump to the right of the cabin chimney. (Ulster Folk and Transport Museum)

and a single one at Port Glasgow, *Glasgow*, and probably *Kelvin*. There was no correlation between the place of build and their sterns, except the Greenock gabberts were all square sterned. All except one were owned in Glasgow and most were in the hands of merchants. The *Glasgow* of 1807 was owned by her skipper, the curiously-named Wardrope Patterson of Glasgow, and the *Christiana* of 1803 was owned by Thomas Hastings, a Glasgow chimney sweep. Her master was also a Thomas Hastings. This could be his son or perhaps he swept chimneys between cargo trips.

Gabberts were also associated with the Forth and Clyde Canal. Its locks restricted their dimensions to 60ft long and 15 to 17ft beam (*McDonald, 1976: 6*). Stoddart's *Scotch Scenery* of 1801 contains an engraving of two gabberts with square sails near Port Dundas at the eastern end of the canal. There are two much-published photographs of what are believed to be late nineteenth-century examples of gabberts – a time when they must have been pretty rare. The first is that of the *Mary* in the Holy Loch in the 1880s. The second, which is undated, shows a gabbert with a square stern and a bowsprit. She is sitting on the mud at low tide, showing a well-rounded bilge and a flat bottom, near Brodick castle, Arran. (*Simper, 1974: 39–40*). Both showed sloops that were similar to Mersey flats in shape, rig and layout. Even the painting of the mast white above the hounds and the design of the wind vane seemed to have been

Turf boats at Limerick in a mid-nineteenth-century engraving.

identical. The main differences seem to have been more sheer at the bow and two instead of three shrouds supporting the mast. However, the Glasgow Shipping Registers show that gabberts were locally built, and while they had similar length and beam to Mersey flats, they had a shallower draft. If flats were built as far north as Whitehaven and were occasionally owned as far south as the Bristol Channel, it is not inconceivable that they found their way further north. The only one I have found was the *Better Luck*. She was a 67-ton flat, built at Northwich in 1825 and later converted into a schooner for the coastal trade. By 1869, she was owned by Cunningham & Co. at Girvan, to the south of the Clyde.

In the twentieth century, other sailing barges were sold to Scottish owners, and these included the Tamar barge *Princess Mayse*, which worked on the Clyde until 1949, and the steel billyboy *Halcyon*, which was scrapped in 1966. A curious reference to the gabbert sloop appeared in the Robert Davy's memoranda book. In 1817, this Topsham shipbuilder constructed a number of Leith smacks to the designs of the Scottish naval architect, Peter Hedderwick. They were intended for the fast packet service between Leith and London. Davy also built six 50-ton 'galliots', to Hedderwick's plans, for use on the Forth and Clyde Canal, and described them as 'very pritty' (*Ponsford, 1988: xvii, 59*). It is strange to think that a shipbuilder in the South-West of England was building sailing barges for use hundreds of miles to the north. Galliots were normally ketch rigged with square top sails on the main mast. Perhaps he meant gabberts. Five of these were sold at Leith in 1847 when the Shipping Register specified that they had two masts that were lateen rigged (*Nix, 2007: personal communication*). While this kind of triangular sail was common for centuries in the

A Wexford cot loaded with sacks of grain.

Mediterranean, and it had been used on the mizzen of seagoing, full-rigged ships up to the mid-eighteenth century, its use for estuary sailing barges must have been unique in the British Isles. The Shipping Registers were prepared with precision because they were titles of ownership and the registrar was unlikely to make a mistake. Nevertheless, it is very puzzling as to why such a rig would be deployed to the Firth of Forth.

It is possible that the hull shape of the sailing gabbart was perpetuated in the later canal barges which were towed by horses. This was certainly the case with Mersey flats, where new dumb flats were built in the late nineteenth and early twentieth centuries along the lines of their sailing predecessors. Two survivors provide evidence of this possibility. The scow – the local name for the dumb barges – *U66* was an iron-hulled barge built for the Union Canal about 1890. This waterway linked the Forth and Clyde Canal with Edinburgh. Much patched and in poor condition, it is stored at the Scottish Maritime Museum. In 2004, a wooden barge, probably built in the early nineteenth century, was discovered in the bank of the Union Canal near Edinburgh. It was approximately 66ft long by 11ft beam. Only the bottom timbers survived. It was carvel built and double-ended with a wide central keelson and two side keelsons. The frames were also of a heavy section and very closely spaced. It is possible that this was locally built and may indeed have followed the pattern of the older sailing gabbart (*Headland, 2005: 78*).

IRELAND

Ireland had extensive river and canal navigations. But it seems that there were only three types of sailing barges by the early nineteenth century. There were on Lough Neagh and the linking Upper Bann and Ulster Canals, the River Slaney to the south and the River Shannon

The fate of most sailing barges, the ironically named *New Hope* at Hamble off the Solent in 1912.

to the west. Coal gabberds were used to lighter coal up the undredged Liffey to Dublin in the 1690s. Their owners were often in dispute with Sir John Lowther's agent at Whiteheaven, from whence much of the coal was exported (*Hainsworth, 1983: 611*). Unfortunately, his records do not give any detail of the barges themselves.

Boats have probably plied on Lough Neagh, Ireland's biggest lake, from early times. In 1993, archaeologists discovered a fragment of a carvel boat from the Lough dating from about 1720 (*Wilkinson and Williams, 1996: 93–103*). It could have been a fishing boat or a cargo carrier. In 1742, Lough Neagh was connected to the sea at Newry by the opening of the Upper Bann Navigation. In 1794, Belfast was connected to the Lough by the Lagan Navigation. Barges on both these waterways were towed until they reached the shore of the Lough, where they had to sail or use sweeps to cross it. They delivered mainly cargoes of coal and timber and returned with bricks, sand and gravel. A plan (held in the Northern Ireland Archives and dated to 1800) of the Newry Canal that led to the Upper Bann shows a sloop-rigged barge being towed by a horse. Dumb barges which rigged a temporary square sail were still in use on the Lagan until the early twentieth century. They were carvel built with a transom stern similar in shape to that of a Thames barge, and measured 62ft, 14ft 6in beam and 6ft depth of hold. On deck, they had an anchor windlass in the bow, a long single hatch with covers, and a cabin aft. The very low rail supported on a series of stanchions was a particular feature and there was a solid higher bulwark around the stern. A postcard dating from about 1900 shows one of them on the Lagan sailing with a pocket handkerchief of a sail. There were five people on board which seems too large a number for the crew. Perhaps they came for the trip. Three barges photographed at the Sand Quay, Belfast, in the 1930s provide a detailed view of the deck layout.

There was an Act of 1537 to sanction the removal of weirs and other navigational obstacles on the River Nore and the River Suir, to open water traffic from Waterford inland. One of its clauses mentioned 'cottes' as one of the types of vessel that might use these rivers. The word 'cotte', or 'cot', was applied to the more recent sailing barges. These were the sailing barges on the River Slaney which linked the port of Wexford with the inland town of Enniscorthy. Possibly the Nore and Suir had similar barges. The Slaney cots have also been called gabbards, just to confuse things. Sailing barge terminology has never been precise (*Illsley and Roberts, 1979: 86*). Slaney cots (or gabberds) were double-ended and carvel built. It is unclear whether they had a chine or a rounded bilge. It is likely that they were built with chines because smaller fishing vessels, which were also known as 'cots', were built in the same area. The latter, however, had clinker rather than carvel side planking (*Roberts, 1981: 31–35*). The cargo cots ranged from 40 to 60ft in length, and were mostly built at the Wexford dockyard. They had an open hold and were often loaded right down to the gunwales. There was a small cabin forward and a steering well aft. A tanned boomless gaff sail or a lug provided the sailing power, and when the wind failed (often the case in the upper reaches towards Enniscorthy) the crew of two poled the cot with setting poles, walking from the bow to the stern again and again along the narrow side decks. Up to 1934, large tonnages of maize and wheat were delivered by coaster to Wexford. Here, it was transhipped into cots for delivery to the mills at Enniscorthy. Another cot trade was the seasonal lightering of malt from the maltings at Castlebridge out to anchored coasters, which would then take it up to Dublin for the Guinness brewery (*McCaffrey, 1957: 82*). A photograph of barges at Carrick-on-Suir in 1910 showed two barges similar to the Slaney cots, but without any evidence of masts or sails (*Delany, 1996: 73*).

By the early 1840s, the River Shannon was navigable for some 180 of its 234 miles. It was also one of the waterways that successfully pioneered inland steamers back in the 1820s. The early nineteenth-century sailing barges around Athlone were square-rigged and carried cargoes of peat piled high above their decks (*Delany, 1985: 1*). There were also gaff-rigged sloops known as turf boats which conveyed peat from the bogs south of Athlone to the major city of Limerick. The boats were carvel built and most of them were owned by families at Garrykennedy on Lough Derg. This inland port also served a large slate quarry which provided additional cargoes. Records of three barges built in 1797, 1824 and 1873 show that they were between 45 and 50ft long, 13ft 9in to 14ft 3in beam and had a capacity of 36 to 50 tons. Some of the turf boats survived into the twentieth century, and the *Sandlark* was still working under sail (with an auxiliary engine) in the 1950s. After finishing, she and three or four other turf boats were abandoned at Garrykennedy until 1973. The local council decided they were an eyesore and had them broken up, with the exception of the *Sandlark*. She was towed away with a view to restoring her but was sadly wrecked while on passage to a new berth (*Barrell, 1987: 41–48*). Hookers were smack-rigged craft that carried peat to the Aran islands under sail until the early 1960s, but with their graceful under shape without a hint of a flat bottom, they cannot be counted as sailing barges. Old hookers have been restored and new ones built, and there is a healthy heritage fleet of hookers that race throughout the summer.

BIBLIOGRAPHY

Allington, P., 'Trials and Tribulations aboard the River Tamar Barge *Shamrock*', *Tamar*, No.28, Morwellham, 2006.

Anon., 'A Clyde Century (Centenary history of Glasgow tug owners Steel and Bennie)', *Sea Breezes*, vol.23 (new series), 1957.

Argall, F., 'The sailing barges of the Fal', *Mariner's Mirror*, vol. 64, 1978, pp.163–168.

Armstrong, J., and Bagwell, P.S., 'Coastal Shipping', in Aldcroft, D. and Freeman, M. (eds), *Transport in the Industrial Revolution* Manchester, 1983.

Baker D., 'The marketing of corn in the first half of the eighteenth century: north-east Kent', *Agricultural History Review* vol.18 (1970), pp.126–150.

Barrell, M., 'In search of the Shannon Turf Boats', *Topsail*, vol.23, 1987, pp.41–48.

Barrow, T., *The Port of Stockton-On-Tees* 1702–1802, Middlesborough, 2005.

Bartlett, J., *Ships of North Cornwall*, Padstow, 1996.

Barton, P., 'The Port of Stockton-on-Tees and its Creeks, 1825–1861' *Maritime History*, vol.1, 1971, pp.122–157.

Idem., personal communication, 2006.

Benham, H., *Last Stronghold of Sail*, London, 1951.

Benham, H., and Finch, R., *The Big Barges*, London, 1983.

Booker, F., *Industrial Archaeology of the Tamar Valley*, (2nd impression), Newton Abbot, 1971.

Bouquet, M., *South Eastern Sail*, Newton Abbot, 1972.

Buglass, J., 'Boats in a Mine', *Nautical Archaeology*, 1998, pp.2, 4.

Idem., 'Tales from the River Bed', *Nautical Archaeology*, 2000.3, pp.6–7. Full excavation report forthcoming.

Idem., *A Rapid Archaeological Survey of Three Wooden Boats near Victoria Dock, Kingston-upon-Hull, East Yorkshire*, Hull, 2001.

Idem., *An Archaeological Assessment of a Shipwreck at Aldborough Flats, North Lincolnshire*, Hull, 2006.

Carr, F., *Sailing Barges* (revised edition), London, 1951.

Childs, B., *Rochester Sailing Barges of the Victorian Era*, Rochester, 1993.

Idem., 'Portland Sailing Barges', *Topsail*, No.29, 1998, pp.8–22.

Clark, E.A.G., 'The Ports of the Exe', in Duffy, M. (ed.), *A New Maritime History of Devon*, London and Exeter, 1993.

Clark R., *Black Sailed Traders*, London, 1961.

Clayton, H.W., *Annual Register of Shipping and Port Charges*, Hull, 1865 (reprinted Liverpool 2001).

Clow, A., and Clow, N.L., *The Chemical Revolution A Contribution to Social Technology*, London, 1952.

Collard, J., *A Maritime History of Rye* (3rd edition), Rye, 1997.

Colman Green, G., *The Norfolk Wherry*, Wymondham, 1953.

Craig, R.S., Protheroe Jones, R., and Symons, M.V., *The Industrial and Maritime History of Llanelli and Burry Port 1750–2000*, Carmarthen, 2002.

Delany, R., *A Celebration of 250 years of Ireland's Inland Waterways*, Belfast,1986.

Delgado, J.P., (ed.), *The British Museum Encyclopaedia of Underwater and Maritime Archaeology*, London, 1997.

Douglas-Sherwood, T., 'Origins of the Norfolk Keel', *Mariner's Mirror*, vol.79, 1993, pp.346–8. (Note: this contains the plans of the Norfolk keel excavated in 1985).

Duffy, M., Fisher, S., Greenhill, B., Starkey, D., Youings, J., (eds) *A New Maritime History of Devon*, London and Exeter, 1994.

Eglinton, E., *The last of the Sailing Coasters*, London, 1982.

Ellmers, C., personal communication, 24 June 1996.

Farr, G., 'The Severn Navigation and the Trow', *Mariner's Mirror*, vol. 32, 1946, pp.66–95.

Idem., 'Passing of the Trow', *Sea Breezes*, vol.28 (new series), pp.378–386.

Ferguson, Peter, personal communication, *see also* early volumes of *Topsail*.

Finch, R., *Coals from Newcastle*, Lavenham, 1973.

Idem., *Sailing Craft of the British Isles*, London, 1976.

Forte, A.D.M., 'The identification of fifteenth century ship types in Scottish legal records', *Mariner's Mirror*, vol.84, 1998, pp.3–12.

Gibbs, M., Morris, B., *Thomas Rothwell Views of Swansea in the 1790s*, Cardiff, 1791.

Gosney, R. and Bowyer, R., *The Sailing Ships and Mariners of Knottingley*, Knottingley, 2000.

Grant, A. and Hughes, B., *North Devon Barges*, Bideford, 1975.

Green, C., *Severn Traders*, Lydney, 1999.

Greenhill, B., 'Barges of Devon and Cornwall', *The Chatham Directory of Inshore Craft*.

Hainsworth, D.R., *The Correspondence of Sir John Lowther of Whitehaven 1693–1698*, London, 1983.

Hampson, G., *Southampton Notarial Protest Books 1756–1810*, Southampton, 1973.

Headland, R., 'Barge rediscovered in Edinburgh' *Maritime Life &Traditions*, No.28, 2005, p.78.

Hooton, J., *The Glaven Ports*, Blakeney, 1997.

Howard, F., 'Fieldwork on the Mersey Flats Bedale and Sir R. Peel' in Stammers, M. (ed.) *Mud Flats: Archaeology in the Intertidal and Inland Waters Around the Mersey Estuary*, Liverpool, 1999.

Hussey D., *Coastal and River Trade in Pre-Industrial England Bristol and its Region 1680–1730*, Exeter, 2000.

Inwood, S., *A History of London*, London, 1998.

Jenkins, H.J.K. 'Fenland lighters and their heyday, *c.*1700–1850', *Mariner's Mirror* vol.79, 1993, pp.155_169.

Illsley, J. & Roberts, O.T.P., 'The Llyn Padarn Slate Wreck', *Cyrmu a'r Mor/Maritime Wales*, vol.4, 1979, pp.62_88.

Jenkins, J.G., *Maritime Heritage The Ships and Seamen of Southern Ceridigion*, Llandysul, 1982.

Johnson, C. S., *The Rebuilding of the Severn Trow Spry*, Ironbridge, 1995.

Kavanagh T., 'Upper Dee Sailing Barges' *Bulletin of the Liverpool Nautical Research Society* vol.39, 1995–6, pp.59–63.

Langley, M., *Solent Creeks, Craft & Cargoes*, Midhurst, 2005.

Leather, J., *Sailing Barges*, London, 1984.

Lewis, M.J.T., *Sails on the Dwyryd*, Tan y Bwlch, 1989.

Lloyd, L., *Wherever Freights May Offer The Maritime Community of Abermaw/Barmouth 1565–1920*, Harlech, 1993.

Idem., *A Real Little Seaport The Port of Aberdyfi and its People 1565–1920*, vol.1, 1996, Harlech.

March, E., *Spritsail barges of the Thames and Medway* (second edition), Newton Abbot, 1970.

Marsden, P., 'A Seventeenth Century Wreck in London', *Mariner's Mirror*, vol.58, 1972, pp.134–129.

McCaffrey, J., 'Wexford Cots', *Sea Breezes* (new series) vol.31, 1961, pp.81–83.

McDonald, D., *The Clyde Puffer*, Newton Abbot, 1976.

McElvogue, D.M. 'Cwch Talsarnu: a boat from the Afon Dwyryd', *Cymru a'r Mor/Maritime Wales* vol.24, 2003, pp.41–49.

Idem., 'The Forgotten Ways: evidence for water-borne transport in Nant Peris, Gwynedd', *Gwynedd Diwydiannol/Industrial Gwynedd*, vol.4, 1999, pp.5–15

McGrail, S., 'Romano-Celtic boats and ships: characteristic features', *International Journal of Nautical Archaeology* vol.24, 1995, pp.139–145.

Macgregor, D.R., *Merchant Sailing Ships 1850–1875*, London, 1984.

May, W.E., *Boats of Men of War* (second edition) London, 1999.

Malster, R., *Wherries and Waterways*, Lavenham, 1971.

Idem., *The Norfolk & Suffolk Broads*, Chichester, 2003.

Mannering, J. (ed.) *The Chatham Directory of Inshore Craft*, London, 1997.

Marsden, P., *Ships of the Port of London: First to the Eleventh Centuries A D* London, 1994.

Idem., *Ships of the Port of London: Twelfth and Seventeenth Centuries A D*, London, 1996.

Matthews, M.D., 'Coastal communities: aspects of the economic and social impact of coastal shipping in South West Wales *c.*1700–1820', *Cymru a'r Mor/Maritime Wales*, vol.25, 2004, 56–71.

Murch, M., and D., and Fairweather, L., *Salcombe Harbour remembered*, Salcombe, 1982.

Nix, M. personal communication, 2007.

Norton, P., *State Barges*, London, 1972.

O'Donnell, H., 'Coasting in the Will, *Topsail*, No.32, pp.25–27.

Osler, A.G., and Barrow A., *Tall Ships Two Rivers*, Newcastle, 1993.

Osler, A. G., 'Tyneside's Riverworkers: Occupational Dress', *Costume* (Journal of the Costume Society), vol.18, 1984, pp.74–77.

Idem., 'Boat usage in Northern Britain: some Medieval survivals', presented at *Medieval Europe: International Conference of Medieval Archaeology*, York, 1992 (unpublished).

Idem., personal communication, 2006.

Paget-Tomlinson, E., 'Powder Hoys of the Mersey' *Mariner's Mirror*, vol.62, 1976, pp.353–355.

Idem., *A Complete Book of Canal & River Navigations* (first edition), Albrighton, 1978.

Idem., *The Colours of the Cut* (second edition), Ashbourne, 2005.

Perks, R.H., 'Evolution of the Thames Sailing Barge, An analysis', *Topsail*, No.28, 2004, pp.39–54.

Ponsford, C.N., *Shipbuilding on the Exe The Memoranda Book of Daniel Bishop Davy (1799–1874)* of Topsham, Devon, Exeter, 1988.

Powell, T., *Staith to Conveyor An Illustrated History of Coal Shipping*, Houghton-le-Spring, 2000.

Ratcliffe, J., *Fal Estuary Historic Audit*, Truro, 1997.

Redknap, M., 'An Archaeological and Historical Context for the Medieval Magor Pill Boat' *Cymru a'r Mor/Maritime Wales*, vol.19, 1997–9, pp.9–29.

Renwick, R. (ed.), *Extracts from the Records of the Burgh of Glasgow*, vol.XIII, 1781–95, Glasgow, 1913.

Roberts O., 'The Cots of Rosslare and Wexford', *Mariner's Mirror*, vol.71, 1985, pp.31.

Idem., personal communication, 2006.

Roberts, O., and McGrail, S., 'A Romano-British boat recovered from a site in Gwent', *Cyrmru a'r Mor/Maritime Wales*, vol.23, 2002, pp.32–36.

Rowe, D.J., 'The decline of the Tyneside Keelmen in the nineteenth century', *Northern History*, vol.4, 1969, pp.111–131.

Idem., 'Occupations in Northumberland and Co. Durham 1851–1911', *Northern History*, vol.VIII, 1973.

Sattin, D.L., *Barge Building and Barge Builders of the Swale*, Rainham, 1990.

Schofield, F., *Humber Keels and Keelmen*, Lavenham, 1988.

Simper, R., *Scottish Sail*, Newton Abbot, 1974.

Idem., 'Inshore Craft of the South Coast', in Greenhill, B., and Mannering, J. (eds), *The Chatham Directory of Inshore* Craft, London, 1997.

Sherborne, J., *War, Politics and Culture in Fourteenth Century England*, London and Rio Grande, 1994.

Stammers, M., *Mersey Flats and Flatmen*, Lavenham and Liverpool, 1993.

Idem., 'The Welsh Sloop', *Cymru a'r Mor/Maritime Wales*, vol.21, 2000, pp.55–58.

Starkey, H.F. *Schooner Port Two centuries of Upper Mersey Sail*, Ormskirk, 1981.

Trinder, Barrie, *Barges and Bargemen A Social History of the Upper Severn*, Chichester, 2005.

Trump, H.J., *Teignmouth*, Chichester (2nd edition), 1986.

Viall, H.R., 'Tyne Keels' *Mariner's Mirror* vol. 28, 1942, pp.160–2.

Vidler, L., 'The Rye River barges', *Mariners Mirror*, vol.21, 1935 pp.378–394.

Vine, P.A.L., *London's Lost Route to the Sea* (4th edition), Newton Abbot, 1986.

Wilkinson, D., and Williams B., 'The discovery of an early eighteenth-century boat in Lough Neagh', *International Journal of Nautical Archaeology*, vol.25, 1996, pp.95–103.

Willan, T.S., *The Inland Trade*, Manchester, 1976.

Williams, Alan, *A River Severn Trow at Lydney Gloucestershire*, Ironbridge and London, 1992.

Williams, G.H., 'The Building of a Conwy River Boat, 1685', *Cymru a'r Mor/Maritime Wales*, vol.5, 1980, pp.5–15.

Wilson, J.K., *Fenland Barge Traffic*, Kettering, 1972.

INDEX